D0773175

MICHIGAN

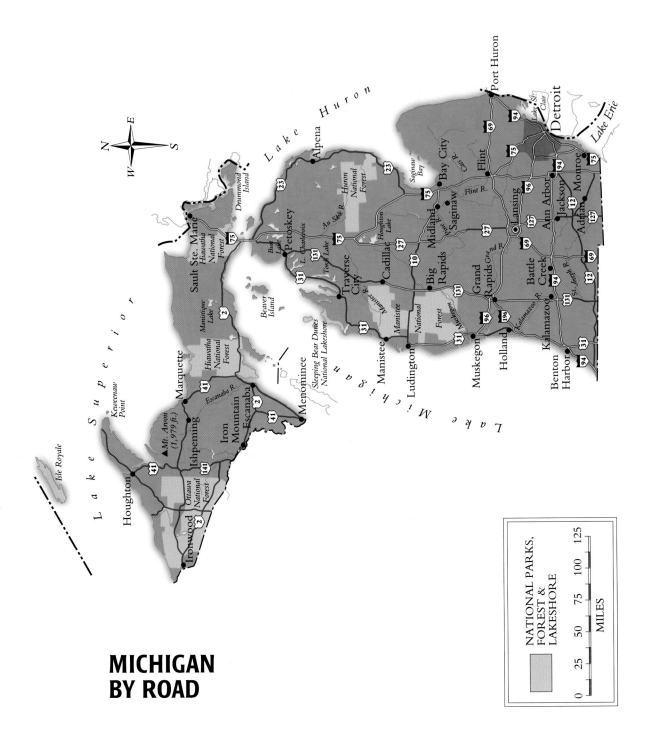

**MICHIGAN
BY ROAD**

NATIONAL PARKS,
FOREST &
LAKESHORE

MILES

0   25   50   75   100   125

CELEBRATE THE STATES
MICHIGAN

Marlene Targ Brill

***B*ENCHMARK *B*OOKS**

MARSHALL CAVENDISH
NEW YORK

Benchmark Books
Marshall Cavendish Corporation
99 White Plains Road
Tarrytown, New York 10591-9001

Library of Congress Cataloging-in-Publication Data
Brill, Marlene Targ.
Michigan / by Marlene Targ Brill.
p.   cm. — (Celebrate the states)
Includes bibliographical references and index.
Summary: Describes the geography, history, government, people,
and culture of this state of many contrasts.
ISBN 0-7614-0418-X (lib. bdg.)
1. Michigan—Juvenile literature. [1. Michigan.] I. Title. II. Series.
F566.3.B75   1998   977.4—dc21   97-5797   CIP   AC

Maps and graphics supplied by Oxford Cartographers, Oxford, England

Photo Research by Ellen Barrett Dudley and Matthew J. Dudley

Cover Photo: Dembinsky Photo Association/Dan Dempster

The photographs in this book are used by permission and through the courtesy of: *Dembinsky Photo Association*: Rod Planck, 6-7; George E. Stewart, 17; John Mielcarek, 19; Mike Barlow, 19(inset); Carl R. Sams II, 20; Gary Bublitz, 24, 72-73, 79, 84, 88-89, 119; Duane Dinse, 67; Ron Goulet, 68, 129; Dan Dempster, 104-105; David F. Wisse, 111; Mark E. Gibson, 116; Joey Sroka, back cover. *Photo Researchers, Inc.*: Tom Hollyman, 10-11; Joseph Nettis, 15; Tim Davis, 21; Rod Planck, 22; George Haling, 62, 127; David R. Frazier, 75(top); Jeff Lapore, 124(right); Renee Lynn, 124(left). *Michigan Jobs Commission/Michigan Travel Bureau*: 13, 54- 55, 66, 70, 78, 107, 121. *The Grand Rapids Art Museum/Gift of Mrs. Nell Drew in memory of Walter Drew*: 28-29. *National Museau of American Art/Art Resource-Gift of Mrs. Joseph Harrison Jr.*: 31. *Courtesy of David Walker, St.Ignace/Photo courtesy Kresge Art Museum*: 34. *Michigan Capitol Collection*: 35, 37. *Gift of the Fred Sanders Company in memory of its founder, Fred Sanders Photograph c 1997 The Detroit Institute of Arts*: 39. *Bayliss Public Library, Sault Ste. Marie*: 44. *State Archives Michigan, Department of State*: 47. *Grand Rapids Public Library*: 49. *Burton Historical Collection, Detroit Public Library*: 52. *Office of the Governor of the State of Michigan*: 58. *Michigan State Fair/Elaine M. Hercock*: 64. *Corbis- Bettmann*:45, 91(left and right), 93, 131(top), 132(top), 134. *Reuters/Corbis-Bettmann*: 60, 131(left), 136. *The Image Bank*: Robin Forbes, 75 (bottom), Gary Cralle, 100. *UPI/Corbis- Bettmann*: 80, 81, 94, 96(left and right), 103, 132(bottom), 133(left and right), 135; James P. Rowen: 83, 108, 114. *InterlockenCenter for the Arts/David Speckman*: 86. *Reuters/Archive Photos*: Sue Ogocki, 97; Fred Prouser, 102. *Courtesy of Dorothy Nathan*: 92. *Muskegon Museum of Art/Courtesy of Mrs. and Mr. Jon Keene*: 98. *Gift of Edsel B. Ford, Ford Motor Company, c 1997 The Detroit Institute of Arts*: 110.

Printed in Italy

1   3   5   6   4   2

CONTENTS

MICHIGAN IS . . . .

Michigan is fruitful land . . .

"Such an abundance of wild strawberries, raspberries and black-berries that they fairly perfumed the air of the whole coast"
—Ottawa chief Andrew Blackbird

"Men who looked about them saw the pines on the Muskegon . . . on the immense web of the Saginaw River system. . . .The boom was on."
—Historian Bruce Catton

. . . and clever people.

"I was to build one carriage in as nearly perfect a manner as possible."
—Pioneer automobile maker Ransom Olds

"I am learning that you can create art from yourself."
—Twelve-year-old Interlochen camper

Its residents came from many lands . . .

"I was lucky to grow up in Michigan, with its great cross-section of people. . . . The diversity of religions, race, and ethnic background exposed me to the world itself."
—President Gerald Ford

"How beautiful we are in our diversity, borne here and cradled by the earth."
—Beaver Island author Mary Blocksma

. . . flourished in their new home . . .

"I am in a country . . . where everyone speaks of the past with triumph, the present with delight, the future with growing confidence."   —An English settler

. . . and changed the world.

"We must recognize there are other disadvantaged people. . . . What we're talking about is [fostering] peaceful social change."
                                    —Union leader Walter Reuther

---

Michigan is a crazy quilt of contrasts. It is rolling farmland, giant factories, and endless forests. It is lively campus towns, old mining and lumber camps, and quiet villages. Hard-working immigrants built each community, turning land into goods that have made America proud. But Michigan hides most of its treasures. They lie down back roads or behind closed doors on city streets. Once discovered, however, communities spring to life with colorful histories and interesting people and many surprises. This is Michigan's story.

1 THE WOLVERINE STATE

Sparkling waterfalls, thick forests, unusual rocks, wildlife—Michigan's natural wonders have been the subject of stories and poems since before the written word. The outdoor Michigan we know began forming about two million years ago.

Back then, large sections of the state shifted from land to water and back again. Prehistoric plants and animals lived and died as the earth changed.

More than one million years later, slabs of ice, or glaciers, crept across the region. Four different glaciers ground the rock piles into lowland and swamps. They carved valleys and deep lake beds. As time passed, the earth kept its richness. The lake and river beds filled. And people from everywhere were drawn to Michigan's land and waters.

TWO WORLDS

The last glacier to cover Michigan divided the region into two peninsulas, land masses with water on three sides. The clear blue Straits of Mackinac separate the peninsulas. Dozens of islands near Michigan's shores became part of the state as well. Each area delighted newcomers with a wealth of wild treasures. The varied beauty inspired future lawmakers to create the state motto: "If you seek a pleasant peninsula, look about you."

The trip between Michigan's peninsulas—now a ten-minute drive across the Mackinac Bridge—once took an entire day by ferry.

Today, the mitten-shaped Lower Peninsula points its rounded hand north toward Canada. Waterways to the northeast form a "thumb." Indiana and Ohio to the south are the only states along the Lower Peninsula border. The only state bordering the Upper Peninsula, or UP, is Wisconsin, which runs along its southwest rim.

The Mackinac Bridge, one of the world's longest suspension bridges, joins the two peninsulas. With two peninsulas and some two hundred nearby islands, Michigan seems spread out. But its size ranks just twenty-third among the United States.

Besides its neighbor states, Michigan connects with another country—Canada. Each day drivers rush across the Ambassador Bridge over the Detroit River between downtown Detroit and Windsor, Ontario, or hurry through the underwater Detroit-Windsor Tunnel. This is the only place along the nation's border where Canada lies south of the United States.

MICHIGAMA

Michigan's main attractions have always been its waterways. Upon entering the Great Lakes, explorer Henry Schoolcraft wrote, "He who, for the first time, lifts his eyes upon this expanse, is amazed and delighted at its magnitude." As the glaciers melted, they left Michigan bounded by four of the five Great Lakes. Lake Huron lies to the east, Lake Erie to the southeast, Lake Superior to the north, and Lake Michigan to the west. The Great Lakes are the largest bodies of inland water in the world. They have affected ways of life in Michigan for centuries. Even the state name comes from the Ojibwa word *michigama*, meaning "great water."

Waves from these lakes crash onto three-quarters of the state's border. Michigan beaches are longer than those of any state except Alaska. They create the largest fresh water sand dunes in the world. Some say they are also the most beautiful. Sandy floors anchor forests in the Upper Peninsula. Farther south, wavy grasses cover many of the dunes.

At Sleeping Bear Dunes National Lakeshore in the Lower Peninsula, sand mounds reach four hundred feet high. Ojibwa legend says that the largest dune represents a sleeping mother bear. "Dunes can originate from different sources," park interpreter Alan Wernette explains. "At Sleeping Bear, the sand came from glaciers. Black bits in the fine sand are iron, a mineral not found in this region. Glaciers must have migrated from ancient mountains north of the UP."

Sometimes, signs of life from long ago lie under the dunes. No

Climbers scramble up the steep sand bluffs at Sleeping Bear Dunes National Lakeshore.

one knows how fossils of three ocean-swimming whales wound up in Tecumseh, Flint, and Oscoda. Geologists believe they swam up prehistoric lakes that no longer exist. The whales became stranded in the shallow waters and died, leaving their skeletons buried in the sand.

WATER WONDERLAND

Glaciers formed over eleven thousand lakes in Michigan. Countless streams extend into forests and farmland. Michigan claims more fresh water than any other state. No wonder it became known as the "Water Wonderland."

The Upper Peninsula is waterfall country. Over 150 waterfalls plunge into the UP's many rivers and streams. The most famous is Tahquamenon Falls, which is two hundred feet across and has a fifty-foot drop. It is the second-largest waterfall in the United States east of the Mississippi River and uses the second-greatest amount of water. Easterner Henry Wadsworth Longfellow was so taken with the falls he wrote about it in his poem "The Song of Hiawatha."

Central Michigan is home to Houghton Lake, the state's largest inland lake. Three other important waterways, the Grand, Kalamazoo, and Saginaw Rivers, flow into the Great Lakes from the heart of lower Michigan. These water routes helped make Michigan a thriving logging state during the late 1800s.

The sands near the mouth of the Kalamazoo hide a famous

Michigan's largest waterfall, Tahquamenon Falls, splashes into a scenic state park.

Michigan ghost town called Singapore. The town was founded in the 1830s and grew to rival Chicago and Milwaukee as a lake port. By the 1870s, Singapore developed into a busy lumber town with three mills, two hotels, a bank, and many general stores. Once the lumber supply disappeared, the bustling waterfront harbor died. Folks moved north to livelier Saugatuck. Over time, Lake Michigan's shifting sands buried Singapore. Today, the town is remembered by a plaque overlooking Saugatuck Harbor.

FORESTS, ROCKS, AND ROLLING HILLS

Immigrants often found what they were looking for in Michigan— a place to remind them of home. Perhaps cold, forested northern hills recalled Finland. Or flat Lower Michigan suggested Dutch tulip and celery fields. As Michigan geologist Steve Wilson noted, "If you can't find it here, it doesn't exist!"

Much of the Upper Peninsula is forest. North of Grayling, some trees stand 150 feet tall and are three hundred years old. Before logging, pine trees dominated the peninsula. Now many pines have been replaced with white birch, maple, and beech trees. "In spots, trees are so thick sunlight never reaches the ground," one traveler noted.

Thick forest hides white-tailed deer from black bears, coyotes, timber wolves, and an increasing number of sport hunters. Wolverines, which gave Michigan its nickname, never lived in the state. Scientists believe traders brought their bushy-tailed pelts from Canada to trade. For some reason, the name stuck.

Beavers, otters, raccoons, and foxes roam freely through the many state and federal parks and forests of both peninsulas. Some scour endless streams for trout, walleye, and northern pike. Others gnaw on acorns, mushrooms, and blueberries, which often out-number wild flowers on the plains. Fur-bearing animals first lured

Beavers munch on shrubs ashore.

Beaver dams can grow to more than a thousand feet long.

MANAGING DEER

Before Europeans settled in the state, large numbers of deer gathered among the Lower Peninsula's wetlands, bogs, and forests where food was plentiful. Then settlers and farmers cleared southern Michigan. By 1870, most deer had headed north, where they found food in the open spaces and brush left after logging. Within ten years, the northern herd had multiplied to about two hundred thousand deer.

Lawmakers realized something must be done to control the number of deer—for the sake of the deer and surrounding communities. They passed laws to either shorten or lengthen deer hunting season, depending upon the nearby herd's size. Some limited the number of deer killed per hunt. Still, deer problems continued. As cities expanded, hungry animals roamed through golf courses, airports, and housing developments looking for food.

Beginning with a 1971 law, a new policy began. For each deer hunting license sold, $1.50 went toward buying land. The idea was to acquire areas with enough food and shelter for healthy deer to live. Today, millions of dollars have been spent on improving habitats for deer. But Michiganders received the best payoff. More than 700,000 of the 3.8 million acres of state forest have been paid for by hunting license fees. These beautiful lands are open for the public to enjoy.

Wood ducks fill Michigan's waters after the winter thaw.

fur traders to Michigan. Today, small-game hunting continues to draw visitors.

Tall pines and marshy shoreline help protect the 350 bird species that pass through Michigan. The state was the first in the country to establish a network of rest stops for migrating Canada geese. Controlled nature areas at Sturgeon River and Seney attract many geese, ducks, and trumpeter swans.

Michigan's few mountains rise in the western Upper Peninsula, where sandstone cliffs meet the shoreline. The highest point is Mount Arvon at 1,979 feet. The area's many rock formations create a rugged wilderness.

Underground, the peninsula holds a wealth of minerals. Copper and iron triggered the nation's earliest mineral rushes. Iron mines still operate near Marquette. Limestone, oil, and gas fields contribute to the state's economy, while colorful agates, jasper, and greenstone thrill rock collectors.

The Lower Peninsula reveals many different faces. Michigan's major cities are on the state's flatland. Beyond larger towns lie unspoiled overlooks, sandy beaches, and rolling farmland.

Most of Michigan's farms are in the southern third of the mitten. Fruit orchards line the western portion of Interstate 94 and the Lake Michigan shoreline. Heading north, farms fade into forests, quaint harbors, and lakes. Steep banks climb to three hundred feet on either coast.

Flat farm country covers much of central Michigan.

Famous Illinois-born author Ernest Hemingway wrote some of his best lines near Petoskey in western Michigan. Images of wild game, leaping fish, and quiet lakes surrounded by woods appeared in many of his books. "The woods ran down to the lake and across the bay. It was beautiful in the spring and summer, the bay blue and bright and usually whitecaps on the lake out beyond the point," he wrote in *Up in Michigan*.

Almost two hundred islands in the Great Lakes are part of Michigan. Of these, Isle Royale in Lake Superior is the largest. The federal government obtained the forty-five-mile-long island from the Ojibwa in 1842, because it wanted the copper mines. By 1900, the mines closed, leaving the island's natural harbors and interior lakes to nature lovers. The island is home to almost a thousand moose. Packs of wolves feed on the animals, keeping the moose numbers down.

RAIN, SNOW, SHIPWRECKS

"In winter we ski, ice-fish, ice-skate, and play hockey. In summer, we have tons of festivals," a proud Kalamazoo resident said. "You have four seasons here, which you don't get in California or the lower states."

For most Michiganders, different seasons mean year-round fun. Both Boyne City and Copper Harbor hold snowmobile festivals in mid-March, which is a late snow season in most of the country. Up and down the Lake Michigan shoreline, harbor towns organize Venetian Night boat parades and water ski races in summer.

The state's waterways soften the sometimes extreme climate,

Winter brings Michiganders of all ages outdoors to play.

making pleasant weather for Michiganders. Large lakes tend to take the edge off bitter winter temperatures and cool the summer air. The results are gentle snowy winters, long growing seasons, and great fruit harvests in summer.

Michigan is prone to severe storms. One of Grand Rapids' worst rainstorms occurred on July 26, 1883. Driving rains pelted the city for a record two weeks, raising the Grand River to dangerous levels. Lumberjacks floated their logs downstream in preparation for a flood. In their rush, they caused a seven-mile logjam above a railroad bridge. The jam broke suddenly, sending more than six hundred thousand logs crashing downriver. Every railroad bridge in the city was ripped apart. Brave lumberjacks built boons that stopped the logs just short of Lake Michigan. No lives were lost. But property damage was heavy and the region's logging industry was shut down for years.

Violent storms over the Great Lakes have taken their toll on shipping. Blustery winds and giant waves have downed over six thousand ships. The region claims the largest number of shipwrecks in the world. The "Big Blow of 1913" wrecked thirty-five ships alone. Winds topped sixty miles per hour across Lake Huron, whipping waves thirty-five feet high.

The waters of Lake Superior are the cruelest. Whitefish Point, where ships enter and leave the lake, earned the name "Graveyard of the Great Lakes" for its dangerous waters. The worst storm to date came on November 10, 1975. The *Edmund Fitzgerald* sank seventeen miles northwest of the point, drowning the entire crew. Popular singer Gordon Lightfoot remembered the storm in his song, "The Wreck of the *Edmund Fitzgerald*." In 1995, the ship's bell was pulled from the lake. Today, the Great Lakes Shipwreck Historical Museum at the Whitefish Point Lighthouse displays the bell, a reminder of the brave sailors who lost their lives.

PRESERVING MICHIGAN'S TREASURES

Michiganders are proud of their state's natural riches. Between logging and mining, however, they discovered years ago how easily resources can disappear. That's why Michigan began protecting the environment more than a century ago.

"We haven't had the problems of other states," said Jim Dufresne, who works for the Michigan State Parks department.

LAND AND WATER

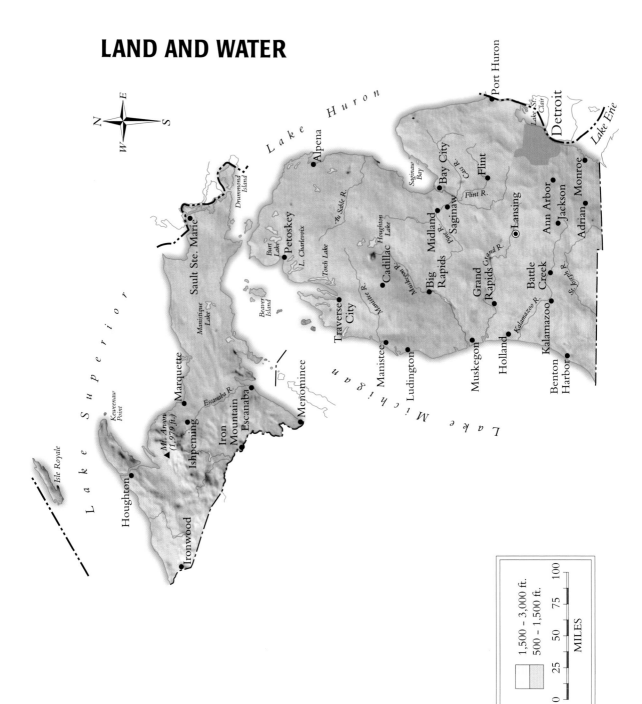

N
E
S
W

Lake Huron

Lake Superior

Lake Michigan

Lake Erie

Isle Royale

Houghton

Keweenaw
Point

Marquette

Mt. Arvon
(1,979 ft.)

Ishpeming

Ironwood

Iron
Mountain

Escanaba

Escanaba R.

Menominee

Sault Ste. Marie

Drummond
Island

Manistique
Lake

Beaver
Island

Burt
Lake

Petoskey

L. Charlevoix

Alpena

Au Sable R.

Torch Lake

Houghton
Lake

Cadillac

Traverse
City

Manistee R.

Manistee

Ludington

Muskegon R.

Big
Rapids

Midland

Saginaw

Bay City

Saginaw
Bay

Cass R.

Flint

Flint R.

Pine R.

Lansing

Grand R.

Grand
Rapids

Muskegon

Holland

Kalamazoo R.

Kalamazoo

Battle
Creek

Benton
Harbor

St. Joseph R.

Ann Arbor

Jackson

Adrian

Monroe

Detroit

Lake St.
Clair

Str.
Clair

Port Huron

1,500 – 3,000 ft.

500 – 1,500 ft.

0   25   50   75   100

MILES

"When mining threatened to flatten our dunes, we passed laws to prevent sand mines. We now plant more trees than we log. We test water and air regularly, especially where we still see problems from large factories."

As early as 1903, the state began replacing forests lost to logging and fires. Twenty million trees a year were planted on private, state, and federal land. Seedlings grew there until age two. Then they were shipped in bundles of five hundred to a thousand around the state. "The large variety of trees in parks came from the hodge-podge of red and white jack pine and white spruce planted since the program began," said Wendell Hoover, a park interpreter.

Mining companies did their part to restore the land. One northern Michigan iron mine replaced an entire wetland that they had polluted with iron dust. Steel factories installed dust collectors to catch chemicals that pollute the air. Water used for energy was recycled. Such efforts have helped provide cleaner air and water for wildlife and Michiganders alike.

Many Michiganders believe that the best way to protect the environment is through understanding. State workers have helped children's museums plan exciting hands-on displays that focus on improving the environment. "We also have major resource centers for environmental education throughout the state," Ron Nagel, a state parks employee, explained. "Each center focuses on a specific issue. At Maybury State Park near Detroit we run a living farm for people who don't know where milk comes from."

Michigan still has a long way to go to end pollution. But educating businesses and families is a major step toward cleaning up the state's cities, streams, and air.

2 MICHIGAN THEN AND NOW

Landscape by Mathias J. Alten

People first appeared in Michigan about twelve thousand years ago. They roamed through the region, searching for food along the lake shores. Ancient hunters trapped mastodons in bogs. They crafted stone spear points to cut the huge animals into food and hides. Others gathered blueberries, cranberries, and tree bark to eat.

About 3000 B.C., the people living along Lake Superior discovered copper. They dug copper mines in the hills of the Keweenaw Peninsula and on Isle Royale. Copper became valuable for making tools, jewelry, and fish hooks. The Lake Superior people traded it to other groups in exchange for shells and hides. Ruins of prehistoric mines still remain on Isle Royale. They represent the oldest metal mining in North America.

Until about A.D. 1000, the people of Michigan got their food by gathering, fishing, and hunting. Over time, farming developed. Women dug soil ridges to drain water and control weeds. Corn and red beans became the main foods of the people of southern Michigan. The ancient wanderers settled on farms. They were the ancestors of Michigan's modern Native Americans.

THE PEACEFUL TRIBES

By the 1600s, three main tribes lived in Michigan. The Ojibwa, Ottawa, and Potawatomi spoke the same language. They lived in

Artist George Catlin captured the excitement of early canoe races in his painting of an Indian regatta near Sault Sainte Marie.

dome-shaped huts of bark and saplings. As the earliest of the Michigan tribes, the Ojibwa were known as the Elder Brothers.

Mostly, the Ojibwa inhabited the northeast and southern Lower Peninsula and much of the Upper Peninsula. The Ottawa occupied the western Lower Peninsula, and the Potawatomi settled to the south. Other nations, such as the Menominee and Wyandot, lived peacefully among them.

Then, beginning in the 1600s, Europeans built colonies along the Atlantic coast. Settlers forced the Iroquois from their hunting grounds in the Northeast. Homeless bands of Iroquois swept

THE FIRST FIREFLY: AN OJIBWA LEGEND

Nana-boo-shoo and Mu-kaw-gee hunted for food in the early days of Mother Earth. "Please fill our stomachs with food and spirit," they begged the first trout they saw from the water's edge. The trout agreed to be eaten. He had always wondered about the world without water. Now his spirit could find out firsthand as part of these creatures.

The Ojibwa thanked the trout and the Great Spirit of water. Then they gathered wood for a cooking fire. As the fish baked, wonderful smells filled the forest. A hungry fly noticed and followed the smell to the fire.

The fly darted among the flames, trying to reach the cooking fish. "Move away from the hot fire," warned Nana-boo-shoo. "We will share when the fish is done."

The fly was too hungry and impatient to wait. He dove at the fish again and again, hoping to get a bite. Each time, the heat proved too much. The angry fly buzzed louder and louder.

Nana-boo-shoo grew tired of the noisy fly and began to wave it away. By accident, he hit the fly, dashing it into the fire.

The fly shot out of the flames and dive-bombed into the creek to cool his burned tail hairs. When his tail no longer stung, he lifted it from the water. To everyone's surprise, the tail glowed on and off. From then on, the fly became a night insect lighting the sky for Mother Earth each summer.

through parts of Michigan. Some drove the Wyandot into the Detroit region, who attacked the Potawatomi and Ojibwa. The calm among Michigan tribes ended forever.

THE FRENCH ARRIVE

The first Europeans to reach Michigan came by accident. The French had claimed land along the Saint Lawrence River in 1604. But they insisted another waterway led to the Pacific Ocean and beyond to China. French adventurer Etienne Brulé journeyed the Great Lakes in 1618 in search of that route. He landed near an Ojibwa fishing camp at Sault Sainte Marie, becoming the first known European to set foot in Michigan.

In 1634, another Frenchman, Jean Nicolet, followed the Great Lakes through the present-day Straits of Mackinac to Green Bay, Wisconsin. Nicolet was sure his ship had reached China. He fired pistols to announce his arrival and dressed in colorful silks to greet China's leaders. Neither Nicolet nor Brulé ever reached Asia. But their stories of Michigan's unlimited furs and copper brought other adventurers.

French priests followed the explorers to preach Christianity to the local tribes. By 1660, a mission had been built at Keweenaw Bay. Eight years later, Father Jacques Marquette established the first French settlement in Michigan at Sault Sainte Marie. Father Claude Dablon reported that the site was the perfect place for a mission, "since it is the great resort of most of the Savages of these regions, and lies in . . . route of all . . . French settlements."

The Native Americans welcomed the early invaders. They eagerly traded soft beaver, mink, and fox furs for European trinkets. They taught French traders to speak native languages and track animals through the network of Indian trails.

More traders arrived to build timber forts near the large Native

Father Marquette learned the Algonquian language so he could teach Christianity to early Native Americans.

American settlements around Saginaw Bay and the Straits of Michilimackinac. In 1671, France constructed the first military fort at St. Ignace and called it by the Indian name for the area, Michilimackinac, which was later shortened to Mackinac. Within twenty years, the fort mushroomed into North America's busiest fur trading center.

The fort's new commander envisioned something bolder. Antoine de la Mothe Cadillac asked the French king, Louis XIV, to build a large colony at the *place du détroit*, the place of the strait. The king agreed.

On July 24, 1701, Cadillac sailed down the St. Clair River to the Detroit River with fifty soldiers, fifty traders and craftspeople, and two priests. There they built Fort Ponchartrain from logs and dirt. Cadillac and his chief lieutenant sent for their wives, the first European women to live in Michigan. Ottawa, Huron, Ojibwa, and Miami villages moved near the fort. Soon Fort Ponchartrain flowered into a lively settlement to rival Michilimackinac. Cadillac's

Cadillac told French king Louis XIV that the banks of the Detroit River are "so fertile and so beautiful that it may justly be called the earthly paradise of North America."

wilderness village eventually became the city of Detroit, the future industrial giant.

After Cadillac's success, France decided to expand its settlements in Michigan. The king offered anyone relocating to Detroit a cow, a pig, a wagon, a patch of land, and some farm tools. Farms sprouted on the west bank of the Detroit River. Fifty families moved further west to Fort St. Joseph along the Kankakee River in what became a fruit-growing belt. "The finest vines, the richest district in all that country," one settler wrote.

WINDS OF CHANGE

The fur trade threatened the Native American way of life. As Indian hunters sought more furs to trade for European goods, many gave up farming and took to the woods to hunt and trap. Increasingly, Indians depended on European traders for their daily needs. Meanwhile, many of the whites who came now settled in the area for good, rather than trading with the Indians and leaving.

As more French and British traders arrived, they competed for the Indian fur trade. From 1754 until 1760, the two nations fought a war for control of North America. Some Indians sided with the French, and the conflict became known as the French and Indian War. In the end, France suffered a horrible defeat. After a century of French settlement, when the war was over, the only remnants of France in the area were French names on old forts.

Native Americans throughout the Midwest refused to accept British rule. The British treated the Indians poorly. They ended the long-standing French custom of exchanging gifts to show friend-

Chief Pontiac meets with Britain's Major Henry Gladwin before the Ottawa surrounded Fort Detroit.

ship. British governor Jeffrey Amherst asserted, "I can by no means agree to [gifts], for if [the Indians] do not behave properly they are to be punished."

In Michigan, an Ottawa chief named Pontiac challenged other tribes to resist the whites and their ways. Warriors swept through Michigan in what became known as Pontiac's War. Forts at St. Joseph, Sault Sainte Marie, and Michilimackinac fell within two weeks. Pontiac stopped at the well-guarded Detroit fort, surrounding the fort for five months. Unable to muster enough men to storm the stockade, Pontiac's warriors slowly scattered to find food. Pontiac left for Illinois country disheartened. His was the last major Indian revolt in Michigan.

JOINING THE UNITED STATES

The British managed to reclaim the forts. But they continued to fight—this time against American colonists. In 1775, the colonists declared themselves free of British rule, launching the Revolutionary War. Although the war raged mostly in the East, the English moved Fort Michilimackinac to an island in the Straits of Mackinac to protect its supplies.

The new United States government created the territory of Michigan in 1805 with Detroit as its capital. When Lewis Cass became territorial governor in 1813, the population barely reached nine thousand and seemed unlikely to increase. Indian trails were too overgrown for wagon travel. The national government dismissed Michigan as a swamp, claiming only "Indians, muskrats and bullfrogs" could live on the Saginaw River.

Governor Cass toured the state with geologist Henry Schoolcraft to map Michigan's future. The two were pleased with the beautiful north woods and welcoming Native Americans. Schoolcraft wrote, "Lake Superior lay before us. . . . The sources of a busy future commerce lie concealed in its rocks."

Cass launched a program to bring more people to Michigan. Detroit, Ann Arbor, Monroe, and Pontiac newspapers published reports of Michigan's rich resources. Within five years, five passable trails extended from Detroit across the state. The first military road, the Old Sauk or Chicago Trail, connected Detroit with Chicago.

The opening of New York's Erie Canal in 1825 offered the greatest new transportation link. Now east coast ships could reach Michigan entirely by water. Detroit ships brought wheat, flour, whiskey, and a new product, lumber, to eastern markets. They returned with crafts-people and laborers to work on the Detroit docks.

Immigrants soon discovered the Lower Peninsula's fertile rolling hills to the west. The federal government sold land at a bargain rate of $1.25 an acre. Eager pioneers cleared trees for farms. These first farms grew into the cities of Kalamazoo, Lansing, Battle Creek, and Jackson, in the state's agricultural heartland.

English artist William James Bennett captured the city's lively steamboat traffic in his painting View of Detroit in 1836.

Greed for pelts soon killed most of Michigan's animals and the fur trade. The state's Native Americans lost their livelihood. The region's European traders simply turned to logging and farming. These new occupations required large amounts of land, which the Europeans hoped to gain by bargaining with Native Americans. "The land is ours," a Kalamazoo Indian told newcomers. "You have no right to hack the trees. Your chiefs are bad."

As early as 1736, pioneers had begun chipping away at Native American land. In the end, the Indians lost thirteen million acres of hunting ground and farmland. Some bands were expected to move west of the Mississippi River. Most stayed, only to be forced onto reservation land thirty years later. Life grew difficult for many Native Americans. To this day, many people on reservations near Saginaw Bay, Grand Traverse, and the UP experience hardships. Yet they have also fought to maintain their way of life.

STATEHOOD

By 1832, the state had eighty-six thousand people, enough to apply for statehood. But a serious problem was brewing between Michigan and the state of Ohio. Both claimed the same seventy-five-mile-long stretch of land called the Toledo Strip. After years of arguing, lawmakers compromised. Ohio won the Toledo Strip. In exchange, Michigan was given the Upper Peninsula. On January 26, 1837, Michigan became the twenty-sixth state to join the Union.

At first, Michiganders found the bargain insulting. The wild backwoods was a poor trade for a port at Toledo. Then geologists discovered large deposits of copper, iron, coal, and salt in the Upper

Peninsula. Cities in the Lower Peninsula looked north for lumber to replace the dwindling fur trade. Hopes ran high that the UP could help Michigan prosper. French statesman Alexis de Tocqueville had visited the north in 1831 and had written, "In a few years these impenetrable forests will have fallen; the sons of civilization and industry will break the silence."

Tocqueville's vision came true. By the mid-1800s, Michigan was the nation's leader in copper, salt, and iron mining and lumber production. Wages of twenty to thirty dollars a month attracted loggers from Finland to the Upper Peninsula. Prospectors and miners flocked from Scotland, Ireland, and Sweden looking for riches. Lumber and mining towns emerged overnight. Farther south and west, towns expanded with sawmills and furniture factories made from these raw materials.

In 1847, the state capital moved to Lansing because it had a more central location. Boom towns created a demand for railroads to transport immigrants and goods. Owners recruited workers from Germany, England, France, and Austria to clear land and lay tracks.

Congress allotted money to build a canal at Sault Sainte Marie. The amazing Soo Locks help ships drop the twenty feet from Lake Superior into Lake Huron. Henry Clay told Congress in 1855 that the Soo Locks "is a work beyond the remotest settlement of the United States, if not the moon."

CIVIL WAR

At the time Michigan became a state, Americans were in dispute about the right to own slaves. Michigan entered the Union as an

SONG: "MICHIGANIA"

In 1916, George Newman Fuller wrote in *Economic and Social Beginnings of Michigan*: "It was exceptional for a settler to emigrate directly from his place of birth to Michigan. He was much more likely to have a number of intermediary stopping places; for example, he might be born in England, migrate with his parents to Connecticut, be educated in Vermont, engage in business in New York, and then spend some years on the frontier in Ohio . . . before finally settling in Michigan." This song traces just such a journey.

For there's your Penobscot way down in parts of Maine,
Where timber grows in plenty but not a bit of grain.
And there is your Quaddy and your Piscataqua,
But these can't hold a candle to Michigania.

And there's the state of Vermont, but what a place is that?
To be sure the girls are pretty and the cattle very fat.
But who among her mountains and clouds of snow could stay,
While he can buy a section in Michigania.

And there is Massachusetts, once good enough, be sure,
But now she is always lying in taxation and manure.
She'll cause a peck of trouble but deal a peck will pay,
While all is scripture measure in Michigania.

And there's the state of New York, the people's very rich;
Among themselves and others have dug a mighty ditch
Which renders it more easy for us to find the way,
And sail upon the waters of Michigania.

What country ever grew up so great in little time,
Just popping from a nursery right into life its prime?
When Uncle Sam did wean her, 'twas but the other day,
And now she's quite a lady, this Michigania.

And if you want to go to a place called Wastenaw,
You'll first upon the Huron; such land you never saw,
Where ships come to Ann Arbor right through a pleasant bay,
And touch at Ypsilanti in Michigania.

And if you want to travel a little farther on,
I guess you'll touch St. Joseph where everybody's gone,
Where everything like Jack's bean grows monstrous fast, they say,
And beats the rest all hollow in Michigania.

Come all ye Yankee farmer boys with metal hearts like me,
And elbow grease in plenty to bow the forest tree,
Come, buy a quarter section, and I'll be bound you'll say,
This country takes the rag off, this Michigania.

By connecting Lake Superior and Lake Huron, the Soo Locks at Sault Sainte Marie greatly expanded Michigan trade.

antislavery state, and many Michiganders played important roles in freeing slaves. Detroit, Adrian, and Battle Creek were key strongholds of Michigan's Underground Railroad, the secret route to freedom in Canada for runaway slaves. Adrian's Laura Haviland hid so many runaways she became known as Superintendent of the Underground.

The Civil War raged until 1865. Of the ninety thousand Michigan men (and one known woman posing as a man) who served, fourteen thousand died. Brave Michiganders captured Confederate president Jefferson Davis. They were the first western regiment to reach the nation's capital while it was under attack. After the war, President Abraham Lincoln declared, "Thank God for Michigan."

FIGHTING FOR FREEDOM

Sojourner Truth, a former slave, settled in Battle Creek during the 1850s. Truth traveled the country bravely speaking to groups about rights for women and blacks, something few women or blacks did at the time. When the Civil War erupted in 1861, Truth wrote a song to the tune of "John Brown's Body." She inspired the First Michigan Colored Regiment of 1,673 black soldiers marching out of Detroit with this moving stanza:

"Look there above the center, where the flag is waving bright;
We are going out of slavery, we are bound for freedom's light;
We mean to show Jeff Davis how the Africans can fight,
As we go marching on."

HORSELESS CARRIAGES FOR THE WORLD

The war created great demand for Michigan's natural resources, and war-time industries helped turn the state's trees and minerals into arms and vehicles. Rapid development continued after peace was restored. Inventive businessmen took Michigan's raw materials and built international companies that produced steel, ships, iron stoves, chemicals, and medicines. Mines and factories competed for workers to fill jobs in these and countless other factories.

New products thrust Michigan into the industrial spotlight. Around a hundred railroad freight cars left Detroit factories each day. Shipbuilding in Bay City, Grand Haven, and Detroit flourished. Wagons built in Flint and carriages and horse-drawn streetcars from Detroit and Grand Rapids were known throughout the Midwest. But the wagons that caught the world's eye were the ones run by engine rather than horse—automobiles.

Several people designed automobiles during the late 1800s, but it was Michiganders who put the world on wheels. And just in time. Logging had almost cleared the state's forests, and the economy was in a downturn.

Ransom Olds and Frank Clark of Lansing opened Olds Motor Works in 1899, the first company to make gasoline-powered automobiles. The men constructed four automobiles their first year, which the public thought would never sell. Unshaken, Olds bought out Clark and continued to improve his line until he manufactured more than five thousand autos in 1904. Olds's factory was the first to build automobiles in large numbers. But they were too expensive for most families.

In 1901, Lansing's Oldsmobile plant produced 425 automobiles, ensuring Michigan's place as a world leader in car manufacturing.

Henry Ford, a mechanic from the Detroit suburb of Dearborn, experimented until he created automobiles the average family could afford. He hired workers who each handled one task of assembling the car. This assembly line system speeded construction, thereby reducing costs. In 1908, Ford's Model T sold for $950, $200 below the average price of a car. Within five years, Ford added a new plant in suburban Highland Park to assemble two hundred thousand vehicles a year. Each cost $550, a record low. By 1927, they cost only $290.

Carriage-builder William Durant added to the growth of Michigan's motor industry. Beginning in 1908, he cleverly bought up and combined several smaller automobile makers, including Olds, Buick, and Chevrolet. His giant General Motors Company rivaled Ford. Detroit was the center of the automobile industry, and factory towns, such as Pontiac, Saginaw, Lansing, and Flint, boomed. Hundreds of thousands of inexpensive gas-powered automobiles pulled off Michigan assembly lines bound for national and international markets. Michigan became the "Motor Capital of the World."

WHEELS OF CHANGE

Cars greatly altered the way Michiganders lived. Automobile factories needed large supplies of iron, steel, copper, leather, rubber, oil, and gasoline. Michigan mines and factories worked overtime, often competing for laborers. Newcomers from Poland, Greece, Italy, Hungary, and Mexico mixed with earlier immigrants on assembly lines. Cars brought the beginnings of suburbs, as roads and highways fanned out from major Michigan cities. By 1920, the state's population soared to 3.7 million people.

The population was shifting from farms to cities. Factory jobs promised fortunes unheard of from plowing fields. Fewer farmers were needed once tractors and other machinery replaced horse-driven plows. In 1920, only one-third of the population lived on farms, compared with two-thirds forty years earlier.

WORKER UNREST

The auto industry's success deeply divided Michigan's rich and poor. Auto company executives lived in luxury and wielded extreme

Some businesses, such as the American Seating Company of Grand Rapids, sponsored classes for immigrant workers to learn about becoming U.S. citizens.

power in local, state, and federal government. In 1953, General Motors president Charles Wilson boasted to the U.S. Senate, "What's good for General Motors is good for the country."

Industry profits often came at the expense of workers, however. Many were overcharged for tools, food, and housing provided by the company. Most suffered long shifts under filthy, unsafe conditions. Bosses speeded the machines to get more work from employees, creating greater danger. When wages increased at his plant to five dollars a day, double what most autoworkers earned, a Ford manager said: "Top management called us in and said that since workers were getting twice the wages, they wanted twice the work. . . . We simply turned up the speed of the lines."

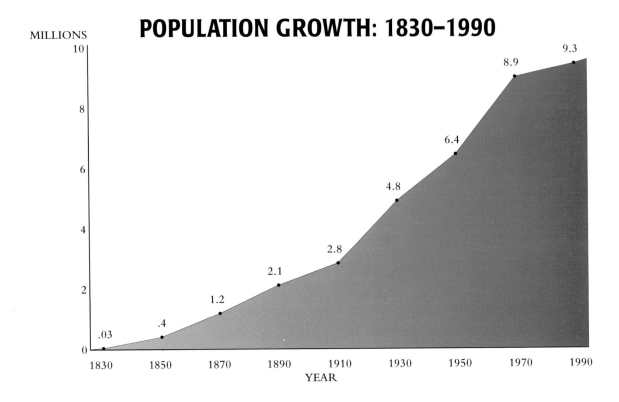

POPULATION GROWTH: 1830–1990

MILLIONS

10

8

6

4

2

0

.03
.4
1.2
2.1
2.8
4.8
6.4
8.9
9.3

1830 1850 1870 1890 1910 1930 1950 1970 1990

YEAR

Workers organized into unions, but auto company bosses refused to talk with union leaders. Then, in December 1936 at General Motors' Flint plant, workers locked themselves in the factory for a sit-down strike after the boss had fired several union men. "The strike has been coming for a year," a striker wrote in his diary. "Speedup systems, favored workers, over-bearing foremen. You can go just so far you know, even with a working man."

Sit-down strikes spread to nearly sixty plants in fourteen states, idling 150,000 workers. Genora Dollinger, a striker's wife, appealed to Flint women: "Come down here and stand with your fathers, brothers, husbands, and sweethearts. They're firing at unarmed men." The women marched with signs and sang until the strike ended. After forty-four days, General Motors finally met with union representatives. Flint became the birthplace of the United Automobile Workers (UAW), one of the most powerful unions in the world.

MODERN MICHIGAN

Union leaders bargained for raises, shorter work days, fairer treatment, and safer conditions. Yet, for years after the UAW formed, few blacks benefited from these contracts. Many southern blacks had come north after World War I looking for factory jobs. What they found were lower-paying jobs under the worst conditions. Some automakers refused to hire blacks or hired them only as janitors. Henry Ford assigned blacks to the foundry, the dirtiest, most dangerous and tiring work. Blacks distrusted the white-run unions and refused to join.

Detroit housing was terrible as well. Former mayor Coleman Young remembered how whites refused to rent or sell to blacks. "The result was overcrowding in the East Side Colored District, as it was called. . . . Housing was poor quality [yet] rents were two or three times as high as in white districts."

On a hot June 20, 1943, tensions erupted at Belle Isle Park near Detroit. Both races usually enjoyed the park, keeping their distance. That day, a fight began between a white man and a black man. Onlookers joined the brawl. Soon racial violence reached outside the park. For two days beatings, riots, and looting spread until

Shortages of housing and jobs increased tension between Detroit's whites and blacks, which erupted into riots in 1943.

the National Guard was called. When the disorder ended, nine whites and twenty-five blacks were dead and thousands of dollars in property lost. The riots unleashed a rage in blacks that lingered for years. Some say the feelings never really disappeared.

In July 1967, terrible race riots broke out in many parts of the nation, including Michigan. Downtown Detroit suffered huge losses with looted shops and burned buildings. Entire blocks were leveled. Roving gangs of rioters clashed with police and seven thousand National Guardsmen for seven days. In the end, forty-three people died and the damage cost nearly $50 million. "This was a revolt of the underprivileged, overcrowded, hot and irritable who were fed up . . . and finally had a chance to be takers," Young said. This time whites fled to the suburbs.

The 1970s brought troubled times for the automobile state. Gas shortages and serious competition from foreign car makers threatened the country's auto producers for the first time. Michigan's unemployment skyrocketed as factories closed or reduced work forces. Many companies moved factories to states with lower taxes and weaker unions, so they could pay employees less.

Single-industry towns, like Flint and Saginaw, suffered most. People out of work had little money to buy goods. Stores closed and downtowns became eyesores with boarded-up fronts. Detroit, the nation's sixth-largest city during the 1980s, had blocks of deserted buildings.

DAWN OF A NEW CENTURY

Inner-city poverty and unemployment has continued into the 1990s. Meanwhile, local and state governments have scrambled to attract new business while keeping the old. Towns have opened museums, restored neighborhoods, and built nature centers to attract tourists.

Michigan has had severe setbacks, but it's not down yet. Its cities are still hubs of manufacturing. Natural resources are plentiful. Moreover, this is a state with spirit, a fighting spirit that recalls the word *Tuebor* on the state flag, which is Latin for "I will defend."

3 THE WHEELS OF PROGRESS

State capitol in Lansing

Few states grapple with the extremes found in Michigan. State government must continually balance the interests of big businesses, strong unions, rural farmers, and everyday city folk. If government tips the scale too far in one direction, loud voices call for change. These outcries, plus new technology, keep Michigan chugging forward.

INSIDE GOVERNMENT

Michigan's government is divided into three branches: executive, legislative, and judicial. Each branch has different jobs. The branches also have powers to check each other, making sure overall balance remains.

Executive. Every four years Michiganders elect a governor to head the executive branch. Michigan's governor supervises nineteen departments, appoints hundreds of people to boards and committees, vetoes (rejects) or signs bills into law, and plans the state budget.

During the 1990s, Governor John Engler tore into the state's sick budget with a carving knife. He reduced government size, slashed state programs, and chopped taxes twenty-one times, mostly in favor of big businesses and the wealthy. Engler credited his tight-

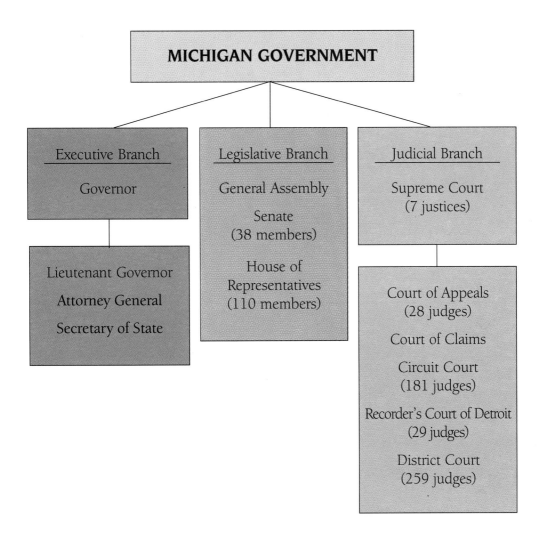

MICHIGAN GOVERNMENT

Executive Branch

Governor

Lieutenant Governor

Attorney General

Secretary of State

Legislative Branch

General Assembly

Senate
(38 members)

House of
Representatives
(110 members)

Judicial Branch

Supreme Court
(7 justices)

Court of Appeals
(28 judges)

Court of Claims

Circuit Court
(181 judges)

Recorder's Court of Detroit
(29 judges)

District Court
(259 judges)

fisted policies with improving Michigan's economy and creating record low unemployment.

His successes came at a great cost to many Michiganders. Without tax money, Engler had fewer funds for social programs, schools, and low-income families. Some people lost food stamps, child care, and health care. The state even cut library and museum hours to save money. By 1997, the state ranked last in the Midwest for quality of life. "Governor Engler has no understanding of kids and

Governor John Engler has made Michigan's economy his top priority.

their different experiences. He has little feeling for the poor," said an angry Detroit teacher.

Legislative. Michigan's legislature is divided into two chambers: the Senate and the House of Representatives. The 38 senators are elected for four-year terms; the 110 representatives are elected for two-year terms. Each represents residents of a particular district.

The legislature spends most of its time creating laws. During a two-year term, the legislature considers between three and four thousand bills that may or may not become law. Bills can originate in either chamber, but they need the vote of both chambers to become law. Once both chambers agree, the bill goes to the governor to sign into law or veto. A vetoed bill can still become law if two-thirds of the legislature vote to overturn the governor's veto.

Judicial. Michigan has a many-layered court system. The highest court is the state supreme court. Seven judges are elected for eight-year terms. Hundreds of judges on several levels of lower courts serve specific towns, districts, or types of cases.

Michigan has one of the poorest public safety records in the nation. The state spends little money on crime prevention. Instead, judges fill state jails with a large number of prisoners. Many people consider Wayne County, which includes Detroit, the scariest region of the state. During the 1970s, Detroit earned the nickname Murder Capital of America. Although the murder rate has dropped considerably, Detroit's image as "crime city" lingers.

RIGHT TO DIE

Many people in politics view Michigan as a trendsetter. In the state's early days, presidents listened to lumber and auto barons. Today, the nation watches what will happen to retired Royal Oak doctor Jack Kevorkian, the man reporters call the "doctor of death."

Kevorkian fights for the right of very ill patients to choose death and the right of doctors to help them die painlessly. Between 1990 and 1997, Kevorkian helped more than forty people die. In response, the state enacted a law against doctor-assisted suicide. Town, county, and state lawyers tried to stop him in three costly trials. Each time juries refused to convict him.

Critics charge that doctors take an oath to preserve life, not end

Dr. Jack Kevorkian has led the fight for the right of doctors to help very ill patients end their lives.

it. They are afraid that some people will choose death rather than become a burden to their families. Supporters argue that people should be able to choose death if their pain becomes too great. Some people would rather die than be hooked up to breathing machines. Many people just want the choice to be theirs, whichever it is. Meanwhile, Kevorkian continues to test legal limits by helping more people commit suicide.

TWO STATES

Most Michiganders feel a strong community bond. Sometimes, local loyalties divide the state. People in the UP feel their interests differ greatly from those of the Lower Peninsula. Every few years UP lawmakers suggest that they form a separate state. They have even thought of the name: Superior.

When efforts to split from Michigan fail, some talk of joining Wisconsin. Many from the UP find more in common with their neighbor than with the rest of Michigan. They claim that residents of Wisconsin and the UP share a quiet, small-town feeling and value their natural surroundings, unlike people in the Lower Peninsula's manufacturing towns. "We have a sportsmen's ethic up here," said Harry Hill, of the Michigan Wildlife Division. "We appreciate nature, being outdoors and sharing and harvesting animals in a fair chase."

AUTOMOBILES AND BEYOND

During the 1980s, Michigan's economy went into a tailspin. As the auto industry declined, so did the industries that supplied its raw materials. Jobs were lost, and with them the salaries needed to buy food and goods and keep the economy moving. Outsiders joked that Michigan's industrial belt had turned into the "Rust Belt."

Since then, Michiganders have been fighting to climb out of the slump. For many towns, the struggle to revive factory, farm, and service jobs has proved worth the effort. By 1994, Michigan's jobless rate fell below the national average for the first time in thirty years. According to *The Almanac of American Politics*, Michigan is "a laboratory of economic transformation, helping show America how to move from an industrial to post-industrial economy."

Automobiles and auto-related industries still generate the most factory jobs in Michigan. But Michiganders learned the hard way

Sparks fly as another automobile receives final welding along the assembly line.

that the state must vary its products. "Technology never remains static," noted General Motors engineer Shirley Schwartz. "Science and technology are like a moving wave."

Michigan remains strong in furniture, lumber, medicine, chemicals, food processing, and machinery-building industries. The state also discovered another natural growth area in recycling. Several paper mills and printers had operated in the Upper Peninsula using Michigan lumber. Once the lumber was gone, printers looked for cheaper and more plentiful fiber. As far back as the 1950s, companies converted used newsprint into usable paper.

Today, almost any paper product can be recycled in the UP. "In 1990, we overcame the myth that magazines and catalogs don't recycle well," said Eric Bourdo of Manistique Papers. "We are the nation's largest recycler of catalogs and magazines recovered from offices and homes. The best thing is we sit in one of the most heavily forested places in the United States, and we don't use any woods for any of our envelopes, bags, or fast-food tray liners."

Some of Michigan's oldest companies have modernized and developed new products. Gerber Baby Foods and Kellogg and Post cereals tempt customers with new taste treats regularly. Dr. John Kellogg and his brother, Will, first invented flaked corn cereal for their Battle Creek health spa in 1898. Recently, Kellogg opened a new research center to study food and health. To honor its cereal tradition, Battle Creek began hosting the World's Longest Breakfast

1992 GROSS STATE PRODUCT: $171.7 BILLION

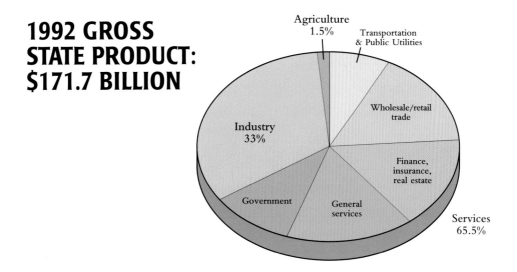

Agriculture
1.5%

Transportation & Public Utilities

Wholesale/retail trade

Industry
33%

Finance, insurance, real estate

Government

General services

Services
65.5%

FUN FAIR DAYS

Michigan has the nation's oldest state fair. But that doesn't mean it's the tamest. Imagine being shot seventy feet into the air in a giant rubber band called the Ejection Seat. Or winning blue ribbons for the craziest parent call. Every year, two weeks before Labor Day, half a million visitors thrill to these and other exciting events.

The first state fair opened in 1849 to help farmers and industrial workers learn more about each other's products. Modern fairs added entertainment, children's events, and livelier displays to the mix. Today, children raise show animals and enter contests to see who has the biggest gum bubble or longest ponytail. This being Michigan, major automakers exhibit the latest car models in addition to farm equipment.

"A favorite is the 'Miracle of Life' birthing exhibit," says Laurie Marrocco, the fair's assistant manager. "Visitors see live chicks, lambs, pigs, and cows being born almost every day at the fair."

Table in 1956. By 1996, sixty-eight thousand guests were downing more than four thousand pounds of cereal each festival.

FROM PLANTS TO FOODS

Food and agriculture are Michigan's second leading industries. The middle Lower Peninsula and thumb regions produce the nation's biggest supply of black and navy beans and cranberries. Kalamazoo, once known as Celery Flats, has become a busy producer of potted plants since the soil tired of celery. Thousands of geraniums and Easter lilies travel cross-country to celebrations each year.

Fruits and vegetables remain Michigan's agricultural foundation. Michigan's fruit belt produces the most apples, grapes, peaches, pears, and plums in the nation. Farmers grow more blueberries, cherries, and cucumbers in Michigan than anywhere in the world. During summertime, carloads of fruit lovers from Illinois and Indiana cross state borders to "pick your own."

Michigan grows 75 percent of the nation's tart cherries. Most come from the northwest Lower Peninsula, making Traverse City the nation's cherry capital. Each July, the National Cherry Festival honors the juicy fruit.

Like the rest of the nation, Michigan has experienced a decrease in its number of farms. Unlike in other states, however, Michigan farmers tend to hand down farms from one generation to another. "Uncle John's apple farm and cider mill is a hundred-year-old family business. Family farms are the norm for nearby mint, bean, and corn fields," said a woman selling cinnamon-laced apple fritters in central Michigan.

BLUEBERRY MUFFINS

Native Americans collected wild blueberries along Michigan shores long before Europeans even knew the Great Lakes existed. Today, Michigan leads the country in harvesting the juicy fruit. An entire industry developed around manufacturing equipment to harvest and clean blueberries. And it's all near South Haven.

To celebrate the tasty treat, South Haven holds the National Blueberry Festival. Each August, more than ten thousand visitors watch the Blueberry Parade, complete with Dutch Klompen Dancers from nearby Holland, Michigan, and line dancers doing the Blueberry Shuffle. Kids compete in blueberry pie-eating and blueberry bubble gum-blowing contests and munch blueberry popcorn. Many take home blueberry plants to grow their own for pancakes, scones, and cereal.

Ask an adult to help you make Michigan blueberry muffins:

¾ cup milk

1 egg

⅓ cup sugar

1 teaspoon salt

½ cup vegetable oil

2 cups flour

3 teaspoons baking powder

1 cup blueberries

Set the oven at 400 degrees. Grease 12 muffin cups. Beat milk, oil, and egg. Stir in flour, sugar, baking powder, and salt until flour is wet. Gently fold in blueberries and pour the batter into the muffin cups. Bake until golden brown, 18 to 20 minutes.

Cherry harvesttime in the northwest Lower Peninsula

To keep their farms, many Michigan farmers require second jobs. Cindy Dutcher raises chickens and organic vegetables. Besides farming, her husband, John, delivers packages. After farming ten years, they are beginning to make ends meet. "Lots of time I worked all day in the field and then waited tables in a restaurant. You have to love what you're doing to be a farmer," Dutcher says.

NATURAL RICHES

Much of Michigan's mineral wealth comes from the Upper Peninsula. Once copper was king. Today, the ore is too expensive to mine. Iron provides Michigan's chief mineral wealth. Iron mines employ two thousand people in Marquette County alone. Only Minnesota mines more iron in the United States.

Construction products add to the state's natural wealth. Michigan supplies much of the country's portland cement, sand, and gravel. Key cement centers are in Alpena, Charlevoix, Monroe, and Bay Counties. Other resources such as oil, limestone, gypsum, and natural gas add to Michigan's income.

Tourism holds the greatest promise as a growth industry. Money generated from travelers to beaches, forests, and parks earns the

With so much to do on the farm, everyone pitches in.

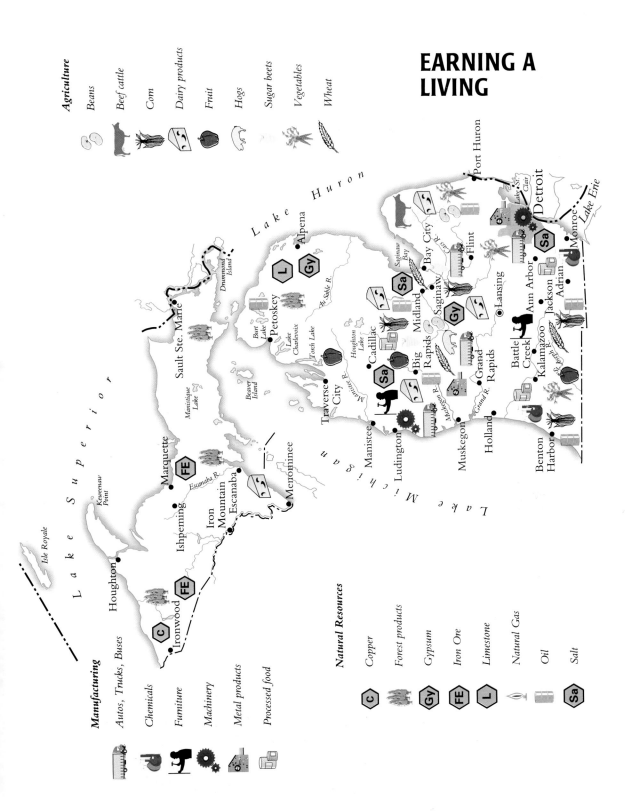

EARNING A LIVING

Agriculture

Beans
Beef cattle
Corn
Dairy products
Fruit
Hogs
Sugar beets
Vegetables
Wheat

Manufacturing

Autos, Trucks, Buses
Chemicals
Furniture
Machinery
Metal products
Processed food

Natural Resources

C — Copper
🌲 — Forest products
Gy — Gypsum
FE — Iron Ore
L — Limestone
🐟 — Natural Gas
📦 — Oil
Sa — Salt

state more than $8 billion a year. Once, tourism was limited to summer fun—biking, fishing, and water sports. Then the state developed year-round activities: trout-filled streams, seven million acres for public hunting, winter sports, and city cultural sites. Michiganders are especially proud of the state's status as first in the nation in number of deer-hunting days. Enough money comes from hunting and fishing licenses to fund most state wildlife programs. All Michiganders need now is a way to let travelers from other states know about the delights of vacationing in Michigan.

Both Michiganders and visitors take full advantage of the state's many lakes and streams, making sport fishing a $1.5 billion business in Michigan.

4 GREAT LAKES PEOPLE

Michigan is a melting pot of cultures. Unlike those in many states, however, Michigan's varied groups tend to divide into pockets. Peninsulas, islands, and surrounding waterways have separated communities. "Overall, people around the state seem guarded about outsiders," newcomer Alison Scott noted. "Maybe it's because towns are so spread out and isolated here."

MICHIGANDERS ON THE MOVE

Ten years ago Michiganders were leaving the state in droves. Young people from the Upper Peninsula migrated south or out-of-state looking for factory jobs.

By 1995, population numbers seemed to be changing. For the first time in ten years, Michigan's population grew faster than most other states. Towns of less than 2,500 people enlarged at twice the rate of big cities. Resort areas in the northwest and western Lower Peninsula accounted for much of the population increases.

"People moving north are older adults who want to retire in these beautiful areas," Trina Williams, of the state demographer's office, said. "People with summer homes here and in the west have decided to stay year-round. I guess everyone likes the slower pace."

Nearly three-quarters of Michiganders remain in urban areas. Most of these people live in the southern half of the Lower Peninsula. The

Detroit's People Mover rings the Renaissance Center along the riverfront, the main downtown business district.

Surrounding Detroit's downtown, neighborhoods decay from a loss of business and a lack of government funding.

difference now is that more big-city folks are moving into outlying suburbs. Wayne, the state's largest county, which includes Detroit, lost 4 percent of its population in 1994 and 1995 alone. Yet Detroit remains Michigan's largest city and is the nation's tenth largest. Add nearby suburbs, and Detroit is the nation's eighth-largest metropolitan area.

"Detroit is the pits," claims one suburban resident. "The city tries to attract people with festivals and new housing developments. Large companies shift from one office building and factory to another. They revive new neighborhoods but leave the old ones a blight. These projects are too few and too scattered to make much difference. People who can afford to, leave."

Indeed, many of the grand downtown buildings are boarded. Mostly, the streets look empty. Several neighborhoods have remained in decay since the riots. Lonely steak houses, Irish pubs, and German restaurants draw only the crowds going to plays at the elegant Fox and Fisher theaters or sports events at the Joe Louis Arena. In 1996, the *Chicago Tribune* reported that Detroit ranked among the ten least-popular cities in the world.

Efforts to bolster Detroit's downtown continue. New office and housing projects brighten the gloomy industrial riverfront. The People Mover, an elevated train, links new sports, convention, and concert halls with hotels and offices.

THE WORLD COMES TO MICHIGAN

Michigan's population includes more than forty nationalities who settled in large numbers during the nineteenth and twentieth

ETHNIC MICHIGAN

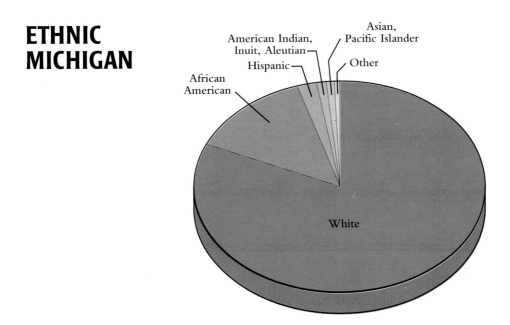

centuries. That means visitors can feast on everything from fried goat cheese, called *saganaki*, in Detroit's Greektown to Polish sausage in Hamtramck to Cornish pasties (meat pies) in the Upper Peninsula. So many ethnic groups enrich Michigan that Detroit holds annual riverfront festivals for each group. Festivals highlight foods, music, dance, and crafts of different cultures.

Michigan's largest ethnic group comes from across the border in Canada. "We also have one of the largest Finnish populations in the United States outside of Minnesota," UP's Eric Bourdo boasts. Other sizable populations are of German, Polish, Irish, Russian, and Dutch descent.

More recently, immigrants from Latin America, Asia, and the Middle East have built communities in Michigan. About two hundred thousand Muslims live in Detroit suburbs, the fifth-largest

CEAD MILLE FAILTE (ONE HUNDRED THOUSAND WELCOMES IN SCOTTISH)

Where can you find boys in skirts, collie sheepherding, and thirty bagpipe bands? At the Scottish Highland Festival in Alma, of course. Each May, the central Lower Peninsula comes alive with music, parades, dancing, and Highland games to honor Alma's Scottish heritage. The festival is one of the nation's major "gathering of clans."

At the festival, dancers compete to Scottish tunes. Some athletes use pitchforks to throw twenty-five-pound bean sacks over a bar. Others toss twenty-foot-long poles as thick as telephone poles into the air.

"What's really neat is the 'gathering of the bands' in kilts, horse-hair hats, and tartan plaids to represent each clan. Colorful drummers and bagpipers fill an entire football field," visitor Robin Campbell bubbled.

"I even joined the Campbell society," Chesser, her husband, an Illinois Scotsman, added.

Frankenmuth is an old-fashioned German town, from the oompah music blaring in the pretzel and cheese shops to costumed dancers during the Bavarian Festival.

Arab community in the United States. Riverside has a huge mosque, and many Arabs cluster in East Dearborn and Dearborn Heights.

"People from countries such as Yemen and Egypt bring large families and very different ideas. Cases of alcoholism are increasing from the stresses of adjusting to western lifestyles," a Wayne County social worker noted.

The state's largest nonwhite minority are African Americans, who make up 14 percent of the population. Most live near industrial areas, especially Detroit. Michigan has been home to some of the nation's most outspoken black civil rights leaders. Yet Michigan remains one of the slowest states to close the economic divide between whites and blacks. According to one study, Michigan ranks fortieth of all the states in offering blacks a shot at economic equality.

One of the boldest black leaders to emerge from Michigan inner cities is Coleman Young, Detroit's first black mayor. The tough-talking mayor saw the city through its stormiest days. He served

Detroit mayor Coleman Young believed "there must be wide-spread recognition that America can only be as strong as its most troubled areas—its cities. There must be a common goal shared between all jurisdictions and races."

Malcolm X wrote, "Sometimes, I have dared to dream that one day history may even say that my voice . . . helped to save America from a [racist] grave."

from 1973 to 1994 and was re-elected an amazing five times. Civil rights leader JoAnn Watson said, "He's the only mayor I've known whom the brothers . . . slap hands and say, 'My man.'"

Malcolm X championed international black rights. As a troubled youth in Lansing, Malcolm Little knew firsthand the hatred of some whites for blacks. His father was killed for urging blacks to end white injustice by returning to Africa. After landing in jail for robbery, Malcolm discovered the Muslim religion and racial pride. Out of jail, Malcolm devoted himself to spreading Islam and preaching violence against whites. He changed his last name to X, explaining that it reflected his lost African family name, rather than the family's slave name.

In 1964, Malcolm had a change of heart. He formed the Organization of Afro-American Unity and called for blacks worldwide to join him in the fight against any racism. He had come to believe that prejudice hurt both whites and blacks. On February 21, 1965, Malcolm was shot, like his father, for speaking his mind.

KINGS, QUEENS, AND CHURCHES

Religion in Michigan mirrors the state's ethnic mix. Roman Catholics maintain large congregations, and a sizable number of Michiganders follow the Protestant, Muslim, and Jewish faiths. Large cities, such as Detroit, Grand Rapids, and Bay City, support this range of religions.

Smaller towns, like Holland, offer fewer religious choices. Many of its residents are of Dutch descent. The town boasts a wooden shoe factory and the only operating Dutch windmill in the United States. The Dutch Reformed Church has dominated Holland since the town was settled in 1847. Holland's Hope College provides education mixed with church teachings. "If you're Catholic like I am, you feel the Dutch Reformed church everywhere," newcomer Steve Eighmey said. "Everyone is open and friendly. But dating can be rough. Parents say 'No way!'"

Michigan has had its share of unusual religions. In 1847, James Strang proclaimed himself "King of Beaver Island," an island northwest of Charlevoix. Strang believed that God told him to establish a strict Mormon community called St. James Village and to take several wives. Some of Strang's followers hated his tight control and he was shot in 1856. All that remains of St. James Village is the Old Mormon Print Shop built by King Strang.

In 1903, Benjamin Franklin Purnell declared himself king, too.

King Ben founded the Israelite House of David in Benton Harbor. Six hundred followers lived and worked together and combined their earnings. They practiced Purnell's strict teachings of no smoking, drinking, or eating meat. Purnell's death in 1927 caused the religion to split into two rival sects. His wife, Mary, established the new Israelite City of David and proclaimed herself queen. Judge Harry Dewhirst led the original group. Both branches survive to this day with about twelve members.

After the two-hundred-year-old, twelve-story-high windmill "De Zwann" (the Swan) left Vinkel, Netherlands, for Holland, Michigan, the Dutch government banned windmill sales outside the country.

"Statewide testing insures that every student graduates knowing basic math and science," says Mary Bailey-Hengesh of the Michigan Education Department.

SCHOOL CHOICES

The newest password to education for Michiganders is *choices*. From big cities to the rural Upper Peninsula, state lawmakers want schools tailored to students and their families.

As of 1996, lawmakers granted parents the right to choose among schools within their school district under the charter school plan. Teachers in charter schools can use new teaching methods.

Many classrooms are multi-age, sometimes having three different levels in one classroom. Students can learn at their own pace. According to Mary Bailey-Hengesh of the Michigan Department of Education, "students love it because they get to stay with the same teacher for three years."

Michigan students receive statewide exams. Grades four, seven, and eleven are tested in math and reading, and grades five, eight, and eleven are tested in science and writing. Tests compare state and regional school districts and help local schools plan better for their students.

After Michigan students scored low in earth science, some creative Michiganders organized school ships, boats that sail the Great Lakes with entire classes. Instructors help students perform tests on the water. They also explain the geography and boating that the students experience first-hand.

As happens nationwide, crime, drugs, and uneven teaching affect Michigan schools. Most downtown Detroit schools have police on campus. About one in ten Michigan families turns to private schools. Most often, the students go to parochial schools. More than half of the religious schools are Roman Catholic.

Two of Michigan's private schools offer some of the most exciting opportunities anywhere in the nation. Cranbrook Educational Community is an art- and science-lover's paradise. Its lovely campus in Bloomfield Hills is home to live-in elementary and high school students and excellent science and art museums that are open to the public. Cranbrook has attracted famous sculptors, architects, and scientists as teachers. Eliel Saarinen, a Finnish architect, designed Cranbrook, as well as countless trendsetting buildings. His renowned son Eero created the St. Louis arch and many world-class buildings and furniture designs. Eero died in 1961 in Ann Arbor, leaving many creations on Cranbrook's grounds and around Detroit.

Another Michigan treasure is Interlochen Arts Academy. Nestled in the forests of the northwest Lower Peninsula, Interlochen is one of the foremost high schools for performing and visual arts. Each summer, boys and girls of all ages can also attend overnight camp. The program blends outdoor fun with music, writing, acting, dancing,

"Interlochen will always be a special place for me and for any young artist who has dreams," says television star Damon Evans, who sang with the class of 1967.

conducting, and painting. "For me, Interlochen was the joy of finding a heart . . . in music shared," said singer Peter Yarrow of Peter, Paul, and Mary.

Michigan has a strong tradition of higher education. The state was the first to establish a college of agriculture—Michigan State in tree-lined East Lansing. It also opened the first college for training teachers west of the Alleghenies, Eastern Michigan University in Ypsilanti. These colleges plus the highly rated University of Michigan in Ann Arbor draw tens of thousands of college students from around the world.

Northern Michigan University at Marquette is the only college to boast a United States Olympic Education Center. The center is home to athletes training for biathlon, boxing, cross-country skiing, luge, and short-track speed-skating. They receive world-class preparation to capture Olympic honors while earning a degree. At the 1994 winter Olympics, athletes from the center earned four of America's thirteen medals. In 1996, they won two Olympic boxing medals.

Boys and girls who hope to win the gold come to the center. Negaunee twelve-year-old Adam Sladek is a member of the Olympic Education Center luge team. He was featured on television's "Get Real" for his competitive spirit. Adam said, "Twenty below, I'm out here. Foot of snow, I'm out here. We're here all the time."

5 FROM MICHIGAN TO THE MOON

M ichiganders have always had a sense of purpose. Perhaps this goes back to the days of fur trading, mining, logging, farming, and then auto building. Inventing new ways to do things was part of each major period, sparking achievements in other areas. Former Michigan governor and U.S. Supreme Court justice Frank Murphy once wrote, "If I can only feel, when my day is done, that I have accomplished something . . . I will be satisfied that I have been worth while."

BEYOND THE STARS

Michiganders have played an important role in the history of flight. Detroit-born Charles Lindbergh made the first nonstop solo flight across the Atlantic Ocean. His airplane *Spirit of St. Louis* soared from New York City to Paris, earning him fans worldwide. He devoted the rest of his life to aviation, science, and world travel.

Michigan claims many astronauts among its heroes. Seven graduated from the University of Michigan. Jackson's James McDivitt piloted the spacecraft that carried the first American to walk in outer space. Another Jackson pilot, Alfred Worden, was command module pilot for Apollo 15, the fourth moon landing. This was the first time astronauts explored the mountain ranges on the moon. The piece of moon rock displayed at the Michigan Space and Sci-

Charles Lindbergh poses in flight gear one month after his historic transatlantic flight in 1927.

Jackson astronaut James McDivitt suits up for training in a copy of the Apollo 9 spacecraft.

FLYING WOMEN

Two Kalamazoo sisters were among the nation's first licensed women pilots to fly military planes. Doris Nathan and Dorothy Eppstein joined the Women Airforce Service Pilots (WASPS) during World War II, flying many dangerous missions. "We were used as utility pilots—towing targets for gunnery practice, delivering planes to squadrons—you name it, we did it," said Dorothy. She even flew the speedy P-51 Mustang that is sometimes displayed at the Kalamazoo Aviation History Museum. "We were patriotic . . . but we were [also] young and looking for adventure," Dorothy remembered. "We had all the adventure we ever wanted flying the latest flyers and bombers."

Ralph Bunche, Detroit's international peacemaker

ence Center in Jackson, a geodesic dome built to honor the state's space heroes, was collected during this mission.

MICHIGAN AND THE WORLD

Detroit-born Ralph Bunche gained fame as a world statesman during the 1940s. He helped found the world organization, the United Nations (UN). While with the UN, Bunche played a role in forging the peace between Arabs and Jews that led to the creation of the state of Israel. His diplomatic skills earned him the

Nobel Peace Prize in 1950, making him the first American black to receive the honor.

Only one Michigander ever became president, and voters never elected him. Grand Rapids' Gerald Ford had been a Michigan representative for twenty-four years. When Vice President Spiro Agnew resigned in 1973, Ford was appointed to replace him. Then President Richard Nixon left the presidency midterm in disgrace. Ford became the nation's first and only appointed president.

"I have not campaigned either for the Presidency or the Vice Presidency," Ford said as he took office as the thirty-eighth presi-

Gerald Ford is the only president never to have been elected either president or vice president.

dent. "I am indebted to no man and only to one woman, my dear wife, as I begin this very difficult job."

FIGHT TO WIN

Michiganders take their sports seriously. In 1997, Michigan had more golf courses than any other state. Biking trails crisscross the state.

Michigan's professional teams generally have a poor track record. Detroit's teams—football's Lions, hockey's Red Wings, and basketball's Pistons—have had few shining seasons. The Detroit Tigers posted World Series victories in 1945, 1968, and 1984. More recently, the Pistons won their only two National Basketball Association (NBA) championships in 1989 and 1990.

Despite the scarce championships, Michigan has produced several stars. Ty Cobb is considered one of the greatest hitters in baseball history. The Georgia-born player, nicknamed the "Georgia Peach," was a Tiger outfielder for twenty-two seasons and manager from 1921 to 1926. Cobb had more stolen base and batting average titles than any other baseball player of his day. His record lifetime batting average of .367 went unbroken until 1962. His hot temper and cut-throat playing remain unmatched. Both were subjects of the recent movie *Cobb*, the story of the Baseball Hall of Famer.

Joe Louis Barrows began boxing in the 1930s under the name Joe Louis. Some say "the Brown Bomber from Detroit" was the greatest boxer in history. He held the heavyweight title from 1937 until 1949. African Americans saw Louis as a symbol of hope during a troubled time in their history. Today, a sculpture representing the

Ty Cobb, "the Georgia Peach," smiles for the cameras in 1915, twenty-one years before he was elected into the Baseball Hall of Fame.

Joe Louis, "the Brown Bomber from Detroit," prepares to defend his heavyweight boxing title in 1938.

boxer's arm and the Joe Louis Arena in downtown Detroit recall his talent.

College basketball hasn't been the same since Lansing-born Earvin "Magic" Johnson left Michigan State. Magic led Everett High School to the state championship. In college, he turned the Spartan's 10–17 record into a winning 25–5 season, taking the team to the national finals. Then, Magic's basketball skills attracted the attention of the pros. After two years of college, he was drafted by the Los Angeles Lakers. There he made history with his 9,921 assists, helping his team win five NBA championships in nine years. "Basketball is a team game, and no one has done more than Magic to help his team win," newspaper columnist Mike Lupica wrote.

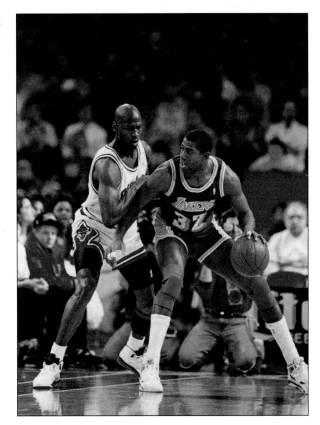

Los Angeles Laker Earvin "Magic" Johnson fends off Chicago Bull Michael Jordan on the way to a basket.

Tunis Ponsen's oil painting Midwest Landscape with Storm *sat unseen for decades.*

SPOTLIGHT ON THE ARTS

Michigan's natural beauty has always inspired writers and painters. But Michigan has never had as strong a tradition of encouraging the arts as some states. Even Detroit's grand art museum displays few local artists. Still, many Michiganders have made outstanding contributions in the arts. They just take some digging to uncover.

For years after his death, more than a thousand paintings by

Muskegon's Tunis Ponsen lay in his niece's basement for safekeeping. Ponsen had won several awards and exhibited in big-city museums, yet his gentle portraits and landscapes never earned the acclaim they deserved. In 1996, the Muskegon Museum of Art arranged an exhibit of Ponsen's artwork in Chicago. His oils and watercolors showed Chicago, where he had studied, and western Michigan at their colorful best. "He deserves to be rediscovered," said Ingrid Lesley, of Chicago's Harold Washington Library, the site of the exhibition. "This is a spectacular show."

Other hidden treasures include traditional Native American arts. Michigan's Native Americans use natural colors and the materials of their ancestors to create unusual textures and forms. Ottawa and Ojibwa artists make baskets, pottery, and quill boxes. The quill boxes come from porcupines that have died along the road. "Porcupine quills are sorted for size and transformed into necklaces, earrings, and boxes, so the porcupine did not die for nothing," said Pearly Broome, who is a "storytelling woman" for the Grand Traverse Band of Ottawa and Ojibwa.

Ed Gray shapes his jewelry, fountains, sculptures, and spirit houses from clay and metal. His artwork has appeared in the Children's Museum of Detroit, the American Indian Community Museum, and exhibits across the country. Much of Gray's art is in copper. He believes copper is a "healing metal given to native people by the creator." Gray learned about copper from his grandmother, whose father also did metalwork.

One of Gray's best-known copper designs is for Red Ribbons of Hope. Gray twists the metal into a ribbon-shaped pin that AIDS groups can sell to raise money for care of patients with this deadly disease. Gray produces about fifty to seventy-five ribbons a day in his Fennville studio in western Michigan. He donates his time, printing costs, and copper sheets.

Since the project began in 1992, Gray has produced more than 129,000 pins. His studio has raised more than $650,000 for AIDS groups nationwide. "People pay what they can for the pin," Gray says. "Sometimes, kids give fifty cents or a dollar. That's exciting when young kids want the ribbon to help fight AIDS."

An amazing collection of plaster casts and bronze sculptures fills a red brick building plopped on the Saginaw Valley State University flatland. One cast is the forceful *Spirit of Detroit*, which

Marshall M. Fredericks's The Spirit of Detroit *graces the city's downtown.*

stands in bronze near Detroit's county building. Another is a thoughtful bust of President John Kennedy. The playful *Lion and Mouse* and *Boy and Bear* add to the broad selection.

All were created by Danish-born Marshall M. Fredericks, who first taught at Cranbrook Academy after World War II. Fredericks's sculptures became world famous, earning him knighthoods from Denmark and Sweden. For many years, he was Danish consulate to the United States. Fredericks still creates wonderful sculptures from his studio in Royal Oak, Michigan.

A WHOLE NEW BEAT

Michiganders tap their toes to every form of music—show tunes, rock, jazz, classical. City auditoriums schedule everything from musicals to symphony orchestras to modern dance companies. Ethnic festivals feature German polkas in Frankenmuth and lusty sea chanties in Lake Superior towns.

Some of the most exciting music to come out of Detroit has been the "Motown Sound." In the 1950s, blacks sang a mix of gospel, rhythm and blues, and popular music in churches and on street corners. Some were lucky enough to cut records. But the companies were owned by whites, who made big money off black music.

Berry Gordy Jr. challenged the system with his budding record company. In 1959, Gordy borrowed money, bought a house for his studio, and hunted for young talent. He called his studio Motown Records, short for the Detroit nickname Motor City. Then he released the company's first national record, "Money, That's What I Want" sung by Barrett Strong.

Motown Records founder Berry Gordy poses with Mary Wilson of the Supremes as the group is honored with a star on the Hollywood Walk of Fame.

Within a year, the Miracles' song "Shop Around" earned Gordy his first gold record. Motown gave Detroit inner-city youth a chance for stardom. Gordy molded his young talent into superstars—nine-and-a-half-year-old Stevie Wonder, eighteen-year-old Smokey Robinson, and Indiana's Michael Jackson and the Jackson Five. "By 1964, most teens wanted blacks singing black songs," says a Motown historian.

Motown's staff eventually grew to 450, overflowing its second studio and the city of Detroit. In 1972, Gordy moved his headquarters to Los Angeles, where Motown expanded into movies and television. Today, only a few singers, such as Aretha Franklin, remain in Detroit.

Still, the Motown sound influenced a new generation of Michigan rockers. A Bay City teenager, Madonna Louise Ciccone, listened to Motown and blended the sound with her own brash style. Then she started a few trends of her own, singing and acting her way to the top of the charts. "I'm tough, ambitious, and know exactly what I want," Madonna once said. That's Michigan spirit!

Bay City's Madonna performs at the 1985 Live Aid concert in Philadelphia.

6 DISCOVERING MICHIGAN

Michigan has a jumble of places to visit—children's museums, space museums, parks, factories, lighthouses, historic homes. Even run-down industrial cities are near pretty hideaway towns and nature areas. Exciting places are everywhere in Michigan.

EXPLORING DETROIT

Detroit sits on a river that connects two Great Lakes and two countries. Detroit's founder, Antoine Cadillac, called the region "the earthly paradise of North America." In 1806, Michigan's first judge, Augustus Woodward, honored the beautiful city with the same layout as Washington, D.C. He built major streets extending from the river through a series of plazas, like spokes on a wheel. Today, expressways cut through the grid, leaving a maze of one-way streets, which make travel confusing.

One of Detroit's liveliest areas is Greektown. Although it is only one block long, its bakeries and restaurants spill around corners. A highlight of Greektown is Trappers Alley. The five buildings lining the alley once housed a fur trading company. Now the century-old brick structures contain shops and restaurants ringing a courtyard.

Belle Isle offers a special view of Detroit and Windsor, Canada, from across the Detroit River. Governor Lewis Cass named the island after his daughter, Isabella, in 1845. Forty years later, Frederick

Young and old bargain for fruits and vegetables at the Lansing farmers' market.

Olmsted, who designed New York's Central Park, developed the island as a public park. Today, Sunset Drive winds through the thousand-acre park to an aquarium, a conservatory, a zoo, and Dossin Great Lakes Museum. People fish, jog, and bicycle year-round. In the summer, cars pack the drive, bringing families to swim, golf, and picnic.

Many Michigan cities honor their farming past with weekly open markets. Detroiters claim their Eastern Market is the largest farm stand in the nation. Open stalls are surrounded by a couple of square blocks of food warehouses and stores with colorful murals.

A 1931 Model A Ford sits in front of an original Ford Motor Company building in historic Greenfield Village.

Every few feet is a different smell—cinnamon, fish, or onions. Visitors can also grab a favorite Detroit snack—Coney Island hot dogs and Vernor's ginger ale.

The sights and sounds of Detroit's car industry are everywhere. Most people here drive, and they drive American-made cars. License plates read "World's Motor Capital." Cobo Hall conference center holds the annual North American International Auto Show, the nation's largest display of cars.

West on I-94 towers a giant Uniroyal tire. The tire began as a Ferris wheel at the 1964 world's fair in New York, carrying passengers in its center. Uniroyal moved the eighty-foot rubber circle in 1966. Now drivers speed by a remodeled tire with fiberglass sidewalls.

Invention has always been the hallmark of Michigan's automobile industry. The Henry Ford Museum and Greenfield Village celebrate both. Henry Ford moved about a hundred famous people's homes and workplaces to a 260-acre lot in the suburb of Dearborn, his hometown. He hauled the entire New Jersey lab where Thomas Edison produced the lightbulb. Ford added a village of craftspeople, a working carousel, and a train. Indoors at the museum, Ford displayed the first motor wagons, steam engines, and farm equipment. Today, the museum also features Motown and black inventors exhibits. All celebrate Michigan's inventive spirit.

LOWER PENINSULA CITIES

Despite Detroit's many sights, some people cannot wait to leave the city. "Everything outside Detroit is really nice and interesting," traveler Richard Benjamin said.

ART FOR THE PEOPLE

As Michigan's largest city, Detroit is the state's art hub. The Detroit Institute of Art is the heart of the arts community. The museum has wonderful collections of early American painters and African-American paintings, pottery, and weavings. But the artwork that really sets this museum apart is *Detroit Industry*, four murals by Mexican painter Diego Rivera.

Rivera completed the industrial scenes in 1933 with the help of Flint's Stephen Dimitroff. The brightly colored inner court walls present life in early auto factories. The bold figures and machines are said to be Rivera's finest American work.

When the murals were unveiled, however, they caused an uproar. Newspapers called the murals "un-American," and said they belittled factory work. Clergy disliked a section that showed a child getting a vaccination. They thought the family in the scene looked too similar to the Holy Family, and that the scene implied that science would triumph over religion. Art critics, however, praised the paintings, and factory workers loved them. Workers streamed into the museum to admire Rivera's account of industrial life. Finally, art presented subjects that meant something to everyday laborers.

Alexander Calder's bright red sculpture La Grande Vitesse *enlivens Grand Rapids' waterfront.*

Many Michigan cities are thriving. With almost two hundred thousand people, Grand Rapids is Michigan's second-largest city. It was named for the rapids that once bubbled through town in the Grand River. Nearby logging made the forested town famous for producing quality furniture.

Today, a series of dams have replaced the rapids. Between September and October, the five-step Fish Ladder Sculpture helps salmon leap over a six-foot dam on their way to spawn. The sparkly riverfront draws crowds for festivals, and the Gerald Ford Museum highlights the presidency. A bright red outdoor metal sculpture, *La Grande Vitesse* (the Grand Rapids), by Alexander

Calder, pays tribute to the river. The sculpture adds to the down-town's lively mix of old and new buildings and industries.

"Midland is the Lower Peninsula's cultural mecca outside Detroit," claimed Detroit's Jackie Pfalzer. "It's a short drive to the wonderful Thumb, where really beautiful lakes and tiny towns haven't lost their old-fashioned charm."

Midland grew up with Dow Chemical Company in Michigan's heartland. Herbert Dow founded the chemical company in 1897. His experiments led to a variety of everyday products, such as aspirin, plastic wrap, and pesticides. Now Dow employs eleven

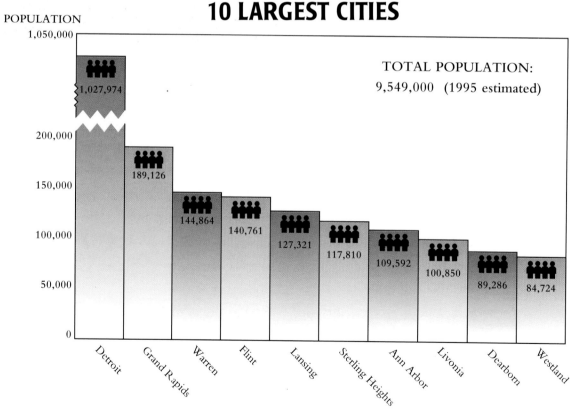

10 LARGEST CITIES

POPULATION

TOTAL POPULATION: 9,549,000 (1995 estimated)

- 1,027,974 — Detroit
- 189,126 — Grand Rapids
- 144,864 — Warren
- 140,761 — Flint
- 127,321 — Lansing
- 117,810 — Sterling Heights
- 109,592 — Ann Arbor
- 100,850 — Livonia
- 89,286 — Dearborn
- 84,724 — Westland

thousand locally, with more plants in Japan. The factory is a town in itself, going on for acres and dwarfing Midland's two-block-long downtown.

Herbert Dow has influenced every aspect of the community, bringing theater, music, and the arts to Midland. His son, Alden, made Midland an "architectural island" with the world-class buildings he designed. During his fifty-year career, Alden gave his hometown churches, houses, and a beautiful arts center. Alden's home has been called one of the most beautiful in the United States.

Near Midland, at the mouth of the Saginaw River, is Bay City. During the 1800s, Bay City was the "Lumber Capital of the World." Today, Bay City ranks among the top ports on the Great Lakes. Its harbors handle more tonnage than any port in Michigan besides Detroit. Beyond the sparkling harbor lie a charming downtown and tree-lined neighborhoods with Victorian mansions built by lumber barons. The most fun hides five miles north at Jennison Nature Center. Here nature trails and marshland are homes to a hundred kinds of birds.

Lansing is Michigan's capital and fifth-largest city. State government takes place here in huge marble buildings. The state library and historical museum share wings of one grand building, providing all the information Michiganders might need. The museum houses such items as the state's first cars and a one-room schoolhouse, complete with copies of old student diaries. The capitol is Lansing's most striking building, with its tall dome. Michigan was the first state to design a capitol similar to the U.S. Capitol.

Few people mill around downtown Lansing, but tucked in factories

Little Sable Point Lighthouse towers over beachgoers at Silver Lake State Park in western Michigan.

along the Grand River are museums teeming with happy voices. The Impressino 5 is the largest of Michigan's many exciting hands-on children's museums. Kids can walk through a giant heart or create magical computer art. Hiding across the river near a car factory is the Michigan Women's Historical Center and Hall of Fame. This museum celebrates Michigan women from long ago to the present.

LAKE MICHIGAN PLAYLAND

For decades, Chicagoans have escaped to western Michigan's resort communities. Artists from every state came to paint the lovely settings at Ox-Bow Lagoon in Saugatuck. Tiny South Haven once claimed more than a hundred resorts. Famous visitors, such as Chicago's mayor Richard Daley, owned summer homes along the coast. Sand, surf, and shoreline sunrises lured vacationers. Quaint shops and beautiful surroundings kept them coming back.

After a long break, the tourist boom is on again. Homey bed-and-breakfasts have replaced older resorts and cottages. The Art Institute of Chicago operates Ox-Bow. Artist colonies dot the coast from South Haven to Saugatuck. Farther north they reappear near the resort towns of Charlevoix and Traverse City.

Each town is proud of its rustic feel and its festivals. "You get three people together in Saugatuck, and you can have two parades," a Saugatuck saleswoman joked. "Fennville has a Goose Festival to celebrate the return of three hundred thousand Canada geese. So we decided to hold a Duck Festival. We have a parade with floats and kids riding bicycles wearing duck bills. It's fun."

UPPER PENINSULA

"We have everything up here," Jim Swede of Copper Harbor said. "We have natural settings and lots of history. There are beautiful trees and rock formations and water."

Between the upper and lower peninsulas is Mackinac Island, "Land of the Great Turtle." The island is Michigan's most popular natural park. Cars are banned, and the only way to reach the island is by ferry. Visitors troop in and out of antique and fudge shops by foot. Residents call tourists "fudgies" because so many stroll along munching fudge.

Costumed soldiers stand guard at Fort Mackinac, looking much as soldiers did in the 1700s.

Many people bicycle or take horse and buggy rides to explore the peaceful state park. Unusual rock formations have such bewitching names as Devils Kitchen and Skull Cave. Arch Rock is a smooth, fifty-foot-wide limestone arch. Native Americans believe the arch is a door for spirits to enter the island.

Mackinac Island is steeped in history. The beautifully preserved Grand Hotel and the many Victorian cottages make it look like time has stood still. At Fort Mackinac, costumed soldiers salute with muskets and cannons. One eighteenth-century soldier wrote, "the air up here is so healthy you have to go somewhere else to die."

The Upper Peninsula is nature at its best. Scattered towns have only a few thousand people each. Fast food is nowhere to be found. Instead, visitors can eat local treats, like Marquette's famous Cornish pasties.

One of the most scenic stretches is along Pictured Rocks National Lakeshore. Pictured Rocks was the nation's first national lakeshore. Towering cliffs and pine forests frame forty-two miles of white sand beaches on southern Lake Superior. The sandstone cliffs soar two hundred feet above the lake and are etched by the water and wind into a variety of shapes and colors. The Ojibwa called the cliffs Pictured Rocks for their awesome colors. Today, visitors can tour the shores, a reconstructed logging camp, and an iron-smelting town.

Each winter, the peninsula turns into a wonderland of outdoor sports. In January, Houghton hosts the Winterfest Snow Sculpting Competition. Mackinaw's Mush Annual Dog Sled Race comes one month later. By then, athletes need to warm up in the National Ski Hall of Fame in Ishpeming, where the nation pays tribute to skiing greats.

Sault Sainte Marie, Michigan's oldest city, is unlike any other town. The city of fifteen thousand is famous for the Soo Locks. The Soo is the busiest and largest link system between Lakes Huron and Superior. Boat tours carry visitors through the locks, sometimes alongside oceangoing freighters. The nearby park has a lock overlook and a view of the museum ship *Valley Camp*.

The Locks Park Walkway takes hikers on a tour of the town's

PLACES TO SEE

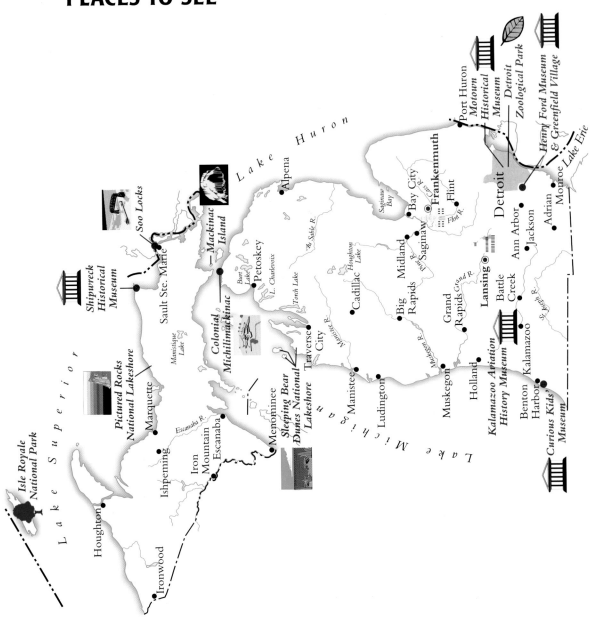

Isle Royale National Park

Lake Superior

Houghton

Ironwood

Ishpeming

Iron Mountain

Escanaba

Menominee

Marquette

Escanaba R.

Pictured Rocks National Lakeshore

Shipwreck Historical Museum

Sault Ste. Marie

Soo Locks

Mackinac Island

Manistique Lake

Colonial Michilimackinac

Sleeping Bear Dunes National Lakeshore

Traverse City

Manistee R.

Manistee

Ludington

Lake Michigan

Burt Lake

Petoskey

L. Charlevoix

Torch Lake

Lake Huron

Alpena

Au Sable R.

Houghton Lake

Cadillac

Big Rapids

Muskegon R.

Muskegon

Holland

Benton Harbor

Kalamazoo

Kalamazoo Aviation History Museum

Curious Kids' Museum

St. Joseph R.

Battle Creek

Grand Rapids

Grand R.

Lansing

Midland

Saginaw Bay

Bay City

Saginaw

Cass R.

Frankenmuth

Flint

Flint R.

Port Huron

Motown Historical Museum

Detroit

Detroit Zoological Park

Henry Ford Museum & Greenfield Village

Ann Arbor

Jackson

Adrian

Monroe

Lake Erie

Michiganders bundle in their warmest clothes to view the snow sculptures at the Winterfest Snow Sculpting Competition.

historic waterfront. Baraga House, the 1864 home of Bishop Frederick Baraga, stands on the trail. Baraga was the UP's first Catholic bishop. But he was best known as the Snowshoe Priest for the way he traveled in snow.

Michigan has many more exciting places to visit. "With 250,000 acres, we have the largest park system in the Midwest," Ron Nagel of the Michigan Parks Department declares. "Twenty-five million people visit each year." And more keep coming. Michigan is a state that casts a spell over visitors, beckoning people back for more.

THE FLAG: *The Michigan state flag has the state seal on a field of blue.*

THE SEAL: *The state seal has a shield at the center that shows the sun rising over a lake. A man on the shore has his right hand raised to symbolize peace. In his left hand is a rifle, showing a readiness to defend state and country. To the sides of the shield are an elk and a moose, and above the shield is a bald eagle. The shield also has three Latin phrases.*

STATE SURVEY

Statehood: January 26, 1837

Origin of Name: Michigan takes its name from Lake Michigan. Michigan is from the Ojibwa word *michigama*, which means "great water."

Nickname: Wolverine State

Capital: Lansing

Motto: If You Seek a Pleasant Peninsula, Look About You

Bird: Robin

Fish: Brook trout

Reptile: Painted turtle

Apple blossom

Flower: Apple blossom

Tree: White pine

Stone: Petoskey stone

Gem: Isle Royale greenstone

Soil: Kalkaska sand

MICHIGAN, MY MICHIGAN

Unofficial State Song

This song was composed in 1911 and has been sung as the unoffical state song for many years. It has never been adopted as the official song because each time the state legislature has considered it, other songs have been proposed as well.

Douglas Malloch

W. Otto Meissner

GEOGRAPHY

Highest Point: 1,979 feet above sea level, at Mt. Arvon

Lowest Point: 572 feet above sea level, along the coast of Lake Erie

Area: 58,527 square miles

Greatest Distance, North to South: 455 miles

Greatest Distance, East to West: 400 miles

Bordering States: Upper Peninsula: Wisconsin to the west; Lower Peninsula: Ohio and Indiana to the south

Hottest Recorded Temperature: 112°F at Mio on July 13, 1936

Coldest Recorded Temperature: -51°F at Vanderbilt on February 9, 1934

Average Annual Precipitation: 32 inches

Major Rivers: Au Sable, Cass, Clinton, Detroit, Escanaba, Grand, Huron, Kalamazoo, Manistee, Manistique, Menominee, Muskegon, Ontonagan, Pere Marquette, Raisin, Saginaw, Saint Clair, Saint Joseph, Sturgeon, Tahquamenon, Whitefish

Major Lakes: Black, Burt, Charlevoix, Crystal, Fletcher Pond, Gogebic, Grand, Higgins, Houghton, Hubbard, Indian, Manistique, Mullet, Torch

Trees: aspen, beech, birch, cedar, elm, fir, hemlock, hickory, maple, oak, pine, spruce

Wild Plants: aster, bittersweet, blackberry, blueberry, chicory, clematis, cranberry, currant, daisy, elderberry, fern, goldenrod, gooseberry, grape, iris, lady's slipper, mandrake, orange milkweed, raspberry, rose, sunflower, tiger lily, trillium, violet

Animals: badger, beaver, black bear, bobcat, elk, fox, moose, opossum, otter, porcupine, rabbit, raccoon, skunk, squirrel, timber wolf, white-tailed deer

Birds: bald eagle, bluebird, blue jay, cardinal, duck, goose, horned owl, hummingbird, mourning dove, osprey, partridge, pheasant, pileated woodpecker, quail, robin, ruffed grouse, snipe, swift, wild turkey, woodcock

Fish: bass, bluegill, carp, catfish, crappie, lake herring, lake trout, muskellunge, perch, pike, salmon, smelt, sturgeon, trout, walleye, whitefish

Red Fox

Barn owl

Endangered Animals: American burying beetle, barn owl, bigeye chub, catspaw mussel, copperbelly watersnake, cougar, gray wolf, Hungerford's crawling water beetle, Indiana bat, ironcolor shiner, Kirtland's snake, Kirtland's warbler, loggerhead shrike, lynx, Mitchell's satyr butterfly, northern madtom, peregrine falcon, Petoskey pondsnail, phlox moth, piping plover, river darter, salamander mussel, short-eared owl, small-mouth salamander

Endangered Plants: American hart's-tongue fern, dwarf lake iris, eastern prairie fringed orchid, Houghton's goldenrod, Michigan monkey flower, Pitcher's thistle, western prairie fringed orchid

TIMELINE

Michigan History

1600s The Ottawa, Ojibwa, and Potawatomi live in present-day Michigan

c. 1620 French explorer Etienne Brulé is the first European known to reach Michigan, when he lands near present-day Sault Ste. Marie

1634 Jean Nicolet of France explores Lake Michigan

1668 The first permanent European settlement is founded in Michigan at Sault Ste. Marie by French priest Jacques Marquette

1671 The French build Fort Michilimackinac on the southern shore of the Straits of Mackinac

1701 Antoine de la Mothe Cadillac builds a French fort at the site of present-day Detroit

1763 The French and Indian War ends; the victorious British take over most French lands in North America

1775 American Revolution begins

1783 British forces remain in the forts at Detroit and Mackinac even though Great Britain has lost the American Revolution

1787 Michigan becomes part of the Northwest Territory, which is eventually divided into five states

1796 American troops occupy the forts at Detroit and Mackinac

1805 The Michigan Territory is created

1805 Fire destroys most of Detroit

1809 The first newspaper in Michigan, the *Michigan Essay*, is printed

1812 The War of 1812 begins; General William Hull surrenders the American fort at Detroit to the British without firing a shot

1813 Detroit is recaptured by the Americans

1837 Michigan becomes the 26th state

1847 Michigan's capital is moved from Detroit to Lansing

1855 The locks at Sault Ste. Marie are completed, allowing ships to travel more easily between Lakes Huron and Superior

1861–1865 About 90,000 Michiganders serve in the Union army during the Civil War

1894 The Kellogg brothers make the first wheat flakes

1899 The Olds Motor Works becomes the first automobile manufacturer in Michigan

1903 The Ford Motor Company is created

1925 Oil is discovered in the Saginaw area

1941–1945 Around 673,000 Michiganders serve in the U.S. armed forces during World War II

1942 Automobile makers switch from manufacturing cars and trucks for the general public to making war materials

1963 Martin Luther King Jr. leads 125,000 people in a civil rights march in Detroit

1967 During riots in Detroit, 43 people die and more than 1,300 buildings are burned.

1973 Coleman Young is elected Detroit's first African-American mayor

1974 Gerald Ford of Grand Rapids becomes president of the United States when Richard Nixon resigns

1976 Michiganders vote to ban throwaway beverage containers; all bottles and cans must be returned for a deposit and recycling

ECONOMY

Agricultural Products: apples, asparagus, beans, blueberries, cattle, cherries, chickens, corn, cucumbers, dairy products, hay, hogs, mink, oats, peaches, pears, potatoes, soybeans, strawberries, sugar beets, wheat

Manufactured Products: automobiles, automobile parts, buses, chemicals, fabricated metal items, iron, machine parts and tools, office furniture, processed foods, sports equipment, trucks, wood products

Natural Resources: copper, gypsum, iron ore, limestone, natural gas, oil, salt, sand and gravel, shale, timber

Business and Trade: communications, finance, insurance, real estate, transportation, wholesale and retail trade

Auto assembly

CALENDAR OF CELEBRATIONS

Ice Sculpture Spectacular Plymouth is home to this icy festival, the oldest and largest ice-carving event in the United States. Every January, hundreds of thousands of visitors gather to watch 200 contestants transform blocks of ice into beautiful sculptures.

North American Snowmobile Festival There's lots of fast winter fun when 10,000 snowmobiles take to the ice on Lake Cadillac in February. This festival features snowmobile races, as well as snow sculpting and sleigh rides.

Irish Festival It's fun to wear green at this celebration of everything Irish. At this March festival in Clare you can march in a parade with a leprechaun band, enter a silly bed race, and dance a jig to Irish music.

Maple Syrup Festival At this Vermontville festival held every April, you can see how syrup is made and eat maple fudge, maple cream, and caramel corn covered in maple syrup. There's also a children's parade and a petting zoo.

National Morel Mushroom-Hunting Festival Tasty, but hard to find, morel mushrooms are the focus of this May festival in Boyne City. Visitors can take part in the official mushroom-hunt competition or just eat special dishes made with morels. Children can listen to a nature talk and take part in a mini-hunt for candy and prizes.

Highland Festival and Games This Scottish festival held in Alma each May features games of strength and skill, such as tossing the caber—a 20-foot-long section of telephone pole. There's also bagpipe music and Scottish meat pies.

Tulip Time Six million tulips are in bloom during this May festival in the town of Holland. Visitors can also view Dutch dancing, street scrubbing, and wooden-shoe making.

National Cherry Festival Traverse City, "Cherry Capital of the World," hosts this festival in July. There are parades, fireworks, big-name concerts, an air show, and, of course, a cherry pie-eating contest.

Au Sable River International Canoe Marathon and Au Sable River Festival An all-night canoe race on the Au Sable River between the towns of Grayling and Oscoda is the highlight of this July festival. All along the 120-mile route, visitors cheer on the paddlers. In the towns, there are parades, arts and crafts, and ice cream and other foods.

Nautical City Festival Rogers City is the home of this celebration of life on the shores of Lake Huron. Visitors can watch a parade, have fun at a carnival, or take part in a beach volleyball competition. There's also a fish fry at this late July–early August festival.

Michigan Festival This ten-day festival in East Lansing every August celebrates all the best of Michigan, from folklife to Native American dancing. Visitors can bring blankets for nighttime outdoor concerts with nationally known acts. A special children's festival features magic shows, music, and dancing.

Michigan Festival

Mackinac Bridge Walk You have only one chance a year to walk across the five-mile bridge that connects Michigan's Upper and Lower Peninsulas. Thousands of walkers, including the governor of Michigan, show up for this Labor Day event in Mackinaw City and St. Ignace.

Red Flannel Festival Every October, the town of Cedar Springs celebrates these red, one-piece undergarments. At the festival, visitors will find a carnival, crafts fair, tractor pull, music, and great food. You can even buy a specially made red flannel union suit.

Color Cruise and Island Festival A trip on a paddle-wheel riverboat on the Grand River is the perfect way to view fall colors during this October festival. On Second Island, near the town of Grand Ledge, visitors can see old-fashioned blacksmithing and wool-spinning and sample bean soup cooked in an old black kettle.

International Festival of Lights Millions of lights brighten the town of Battle Creek during this festival in November and December. Exhibits include Trees Around the World and a giant, glowing Tony the Tiger.

Victorian Sleighbell Parade and Old Christmas Weekend The town of Manistee celebrates an old-fashioned Christmas every December with historically decorated buildings. Visitors can munch on roasted chestnuts while watching the parade, which features horse-drawn wagons and characters in period costumes.

STATE STARS

Ralph Bunche (1904–1971), of Detroit, helped found the United Nations and then served as a UN undersecretary from 1955 to 1971. In 1950,

Bunche was the first African American ever to win the Nobel Peace Prize. He received the honor for helping negotiate peace in the Middle East.

Bruce Catton (1899–1978), born in Petoskey, was a Pulitzer Prize-winning author. Catton won the prize in 1953 for *A Stillness at Appomattox*, one of the many books he wrote on the Civil War.

Bruce Catton

Madonna Louise Ciccone (1958–   ), the superstar better known simply as "Madonna," was born in Bay City. Her videos and concerts made her a superstar, and her ever-changing style has had an influence on fashion worldwide. She has had many hit singles, including "Material Girl" and "Vogue." She has also acted in such movies as *Dick Tracy*, *A League of Their Own*, and *Evita*.

Ty Cobb (1886–1961) played baseball with the Detroit Tigers for 22 years and managed them for 6 more. Considered one of the game's greats, Cobb had over 4,000 hits, won 12 batting titles, and was elected to the Baseball Hall of Fame in 1936.

Francis Ford Coppola (1939–   ), of Detroit, gained fame as a movie writer, producer, and director. Coppola has won five Academy Awards. His movies include *The Godfather*, *The Godfather Part II*, and *Apocalypse Now*.

Francis Ford Coppola

George Armstrong Custer (1839–1876), although Ohio-born, grew up in Monroe. Custer first earned fame as a brave young general in the Civil War. He was later killed at the Battle of the Little Bighorn while waging a ruthless war against the Native Americans in the West.

George Armstrong Custer

Gerald R. Ford (1913–   ) grew up in Grand Rapids and attended the University of Michigan. Ford became a U.S. representative from Michigan and was chosen vice president when Spiro Agnew resigned that post in 1973. In 1974, Ford became the 38th president when Richard Nixon resigned.

Henry Ford (1863–1947), of Dearborn, built his first car in 1896 and founded the Ford Motor Company in 1903. Ford sold thousands of his Model T, one of the first cars affordable to most Americans.

Daniel Gerber (1898–1974) saw how difficult it was for his wife to make food for their baby and decided to make feeding time easier for moms everywhere. He began canning baby food in his father's factory in Fremont in 1927. Within 20 years, Gerber's company was selling millions of jars of baby food every day.

Daniel Gerber

Berry Gordy Jr. (1929–   ), a Detroit native, founded Motown Records. Beginning in 1959, Gordy's company signed a number of African-American acts, including the Supremes, Smokey Robinson and the Miracles, and Stevie Wonder, and turned them into major stars.

Earvin "Magic" Johnson (1959–   ), of Lansing, is recognized as one of basketball's greatest players. After helping his team at Michigan State University win the national championship in 1979, he led the Los Angeles Lakers to five NBA titles in the 1980s. Johnson retired from basketball in 1991 after announcing he was infected with the AIDS virus. He now works to educate people about the disease. He wrote a book for young people called *What You Can Do to Avoid AIDS*.

John Harvey (1852–1943) and **William Keith** (1860–1951) **Kellogg** were brothers from Battle Creek who discovered how to make cornflakes. William began the Battle Creek Toasted Corn Flakes Company in 1906, Which became known as the Kellogg Company.

John Harvey Kellogg

William Keith Kellogg

Charles Lindbergh (1902–1974), the first person to fly across the Atlantic Ocean alone, was born in Detroit. Lindbergh made his daring 33½-hour flight in 1927 and instantly became a celebrity around the world.

Joe Louis (1914–1981) took up boxing after he moved to Detroit as a young boy. The "Brown Bomber," as he was known, became a pro boxer in 1934. He held the heavyweight boxing championship for almost 12 years—longer than any other fighter.

Malcolm X (1925–1965), an important African-American leader of the 1960s, grew up in Lansing. Born Malcolm Little, he became a Black Muslim and changed his last name to X to represent the unknown African name of his ancestors. Malcolm X urged African Americans to be proud of their black heritage and to work for equal rights. He was assassinated after breaking with the Black Muslims and changing his views on how blacks should achieve equality.

Joyce Carol Oates

Joyce Carol Oates (1938–   ) is an award-winning author who taught English at the University of Detroit. Oates has often used Detroit as the setting for her stories. Her novels include *Them* and *Wonderland*.

Ransom Eli Olds (1864–1950) of Lansing played an important role in the beginning of Michigan's automobile industry. In 1899 he started the Olds Motor Works, the first automobile factory in Michigan. Two years later he began calling his cars Oldsmobiles.

Walter Reuther (1907–1970) helped create better working conditions for autoworkers in Michigan and throughout the United States. After moving to Detroit in 1926, Reuther worked to organize the United Auto Workers. He served as president of the union from 1946 until 1970.

"Sugar" Ray Robinson (1921–1989), of Detroit, won boxing championships in both the welterweight and middleweight classes. Often called the best fighter, pound-for-pound, in the history of boxing, Robinson won 174 matches with 109 knockouts, a boxing record.

Diana Ross

Diana Ross (1944–   ) was one of the biggest stars to come out of Motown Records. Singing with the Supremes, she had many hit songs, including "Where Did Our Love Go?" Born in Detroit, Ross went on to a solo singing career, and starring roles in films such as *Lady Sings the Blues* and *The Wiz*.

Steven Seagal (1951–   ) has kicked and punched his way through a number of action movies. A martial arts expert, Seagal has starred in films such as *Above the Law* and *Under Siege*. Seagal was born in Lansing.

Lily Tomlin (1939–   ) is a talented performer who has worked on television, in movies, and on the stage. Born in Detroit, Tomlin began her career as a comedian in the 1960s and won a Grammy in 1971 for a comedy album. She has starred in several motion pictures, including *Nashville* and *Nine to Five*, as well as in Broadway shows.

Chris Van Allsburg (1949–   ), a writer and illustrator of children's books, is from Grand Rapids. He won Caldecott Awards for his drawings in *The Polar Express* and *Jumanji*.

Thomas Weller (1915–   ) is a Nobel Prize-winning scientist from Ann Arbor. Weller won the Nobel Prize in 1954 for his work with the polio virus. He is also well known for his research with other diseases, including rubella and chicken pox.

Stevie Wonder (1950–   ), who has been making records since he was 13, was born in Saginaw. Blind since birth, Wonder writes, sings, and plays his own music. His hit songs have included "Living for the City" and "I Just Called to Say I Love You."

Coleman Young (1918–   ) was Detroit's first African-American mayor. Serving from 1974 to 1994, Young led Detroit longer than any other mayor.

Stevie Wonder

TOUR THE STATE

Henry Ford Museum and Greenfield Village (Dearborn) Some of the best of American history is found at this well-known attraction. The museum covers all aspects of American life, and the collections include such items as the chair Abraham Lincoln was sitting in when he was assassinated. Greenfield Village contains many important buildings from America's past. You can see the home of Henry Ford, the tavern where Lincoln practiced law, and the laboratory of inventor Thomas Edison.

Museum of African American History (Detroit) This new museum houses the country's largest collection of memorabilia relating to black history. Exhibits cover African-American history from the slave trade to the present. Visitors can even walk through a replica of a slave ship.

The Detroit Institute of Arts (Detroit) Art from all around the world is featured at this well-respected museum, which displays everything from medieval knights' armor to African and Native American art.

Motown Historical Museum (Detroit) The great sounds of Motown are remembered in this old brick house where the company started in the early 1960s. The museum contains the original recording studio, as well as musical instruments and other items that belonged to the Motown stars.

Detroit Zoological Park (Royal Oak) One of the largest zoos in the country, this park features animals in cageless, natural settings. Visitors can see such favorites as chimpanzees, penguins, and polar bears.

Lionel Trains Visitor Center (Chesterfield) The Lionel Company's Visitor Center is a delight for model train lovers. The main exhibit features 10 trains running on 1,000 feet of track. A number of other operating train models are also on display.

Michigan Space and Science Center (Jackson) Spacesuits, satellites, the Apollo 9 capsule, a model of the Hubble Space Telescope, and a moon rock are only a few of the things to see at this out-of-this-world attraction. Visitors can also climb inside a space capsule and view an 85-foot-tall rocket.

State Capitol (Lansing) Built in 1879, the Michigan State Capitol was one of the first state capitols to be patterned after the U.S. Capitol in Washington, D.C. A tour of the building's beautiful interior today reveals Civil War battle flags, portraits of Michigan governors, and other items from Michigan history.

Colonial Michilimackinac (Mackinaw City) Several buildings, including a guardhouse, barracks, blacksmith's shop, church, and trader's house, have been reconstructed at this site of a French fort. Costumed actors dressed as British soldiers, French fur traders, and Native Americans help bring history to life.

Fort Mackinac (Mackinac Island) This restored British and American fort features costumed guides playing military music and firing muskets and cannons. There is also a Children's Discovery Room with hands-on exhibits and period costumes for kids to try on.

Marquette Mission Park and Museum of Ojibwa Culture (St. Ignace) A statue of Father Jacques Marquette and a display on his life can be found at this site that is thought to be Marquette's burial place. The accompanying museum displays many artifacts related to Ojibwa Indian life.

Tahquamenon Falls State Park (Paradise) Upper Tahquamenon Falls, measuring 200 feet across with a drop of 50 feet, is the second-largest waterfall east of the Mississippi River. The lower falls are a series of drops and rapids in the Tahquamenon River. Both sets of falls are easily reached along the park's many miles of hiking trails.

Shipwreck Historical Museum (Whitefish Point) Visitors here can learn the stories of some of Lake Superior's 550 shipwrecks. Photos and artifacts present the history of the lake's most famous shipwrecks, including that of the *Edmund Fitzgerald*. The neighboring 148-year-old lighthouse is also open to visitors.

Pictured Rocks National Lakeshore (Munising) The Pictured Rocks of this park are spectacular wind- and water-carved cliffs rising 200 feet above the surface of Lake Superior. Summer activities include swimming, hiking, and scenic boat rides to view the Pictured Rocks. In the winter, plenty of snow makes for great cross-country skiing and snowmobiling.

Michigan Iron Industry Museum (Negaunee) Visitors here learn about the early history of Michigan's iron-mining industry. Exhibits include an 1860s locomotive that was used to haul iron ore.

Spirit of the Woods Museum (Elk Rapids) Michigan's Native Americans and native animals are featured in this fun museum. Native American items such as arrowheads, bows, and moccasins are on display, as are preserved specimens of North American animals including wolves, bears, bison, deer, and beavers.

Sleeping Bear Dunes National Lakeshore (Empire) While this park offers swimming, fishing, hiking, and bird-watching, the favorite activity here is dune climbing. Awesome dunes, some over 400 feet high, make for adventurous, and difficult, climbing. The park's observation platforms offer terrific views of Lake Michigan.

Gerald R. Ford Museum (Grand Rapids) Dedicated to the only American president not elected by the people, this museum includes a replica of the White House's Oval Office as it looked when Ford was in office. There are also exhibits on events from that period, such as Richard Nixon's fall from the presidency and America's Bicentennial.

Kalamazoo Aviation History Museum (Kalamazoo) Great American airplanes are the focus of this Michigan museum. Warplanes and other aircraft from American history are on display, and during the summer, some even perform flying demonstrations. An activity room includes a flight simulator for visitors to try out.

FUN FACTS

If you're wondering which way the wind is blowing, it's easy to find out in Montague. The town has the world's largest weather vane. The weather vane stands 48 feet tall and weighs 3,500 pounds. It has a 26-foot-long wind arrow and is decorated with a 14-foot-long replica of a Great Lakes sailing ship.

Michigan offers a special program for drivers who have a fear of crossing long bridges. At the Mackinac Bridge, which is 200 feet high and 5 miles long, timid drivers can let a state employee drive their car across the bridge while they sit back and close their eyes.

The record for spitting a cherry pit is 72 feet, 7½ inches, which was set at the International Cherry Pit Spitting Championship in Eau Claire in 1988. Contestants from around the world gather for a chance to win the yearly competition.

A lot of Michigan beaches are pretty to walk along; some will even sing to you. The beaches at Grand Haven are one of the few places where singing sand can be found. The tiny sand particles make a whistling sound when walked upon.

Scientists think they may have found the world's largest living organism beneath the Michigan-Wisconsin border. A single fungus—a large mushroom—that covers 37 acres and weighs 1,000 tons is growing beneath the surface of the ground there. The organism may be 1,500 years old, and scientists are not yet sure they have found all of it.

FIND OUT MORE

If you'd like to find out more about Michigan, look in your school library, local library, bookstore, or video store. You can also surf the net. Here are some resources to help you begin your search.

MICHIGAN PEOPLE AND SPECIAL INTEREST BOOKS

Frostic, Gwen. *A Walk with Me.* Benzonia, Michigan: Presscraft Papers, 1958. Gentle poems.

Greenberg, Keith. *Madonna.* Minneapolis: Lerner Publications, 1986.

Greenberg, Keith. *Magic Johnson: Champion with a Cause.* Minneapolis: Lerner Publications, 1992.

Johnson, Rick. *Magic Johnson: Basketball's Smiling Superstar.* New York: Dillon Press, 1992.

Seymour, Tres. *The Gulls of the Edmund Fitzgerald.* New York: Orchard Books, 1996.

Whelan, Gloria. *Once on This Island.* New York: HarperCollins, 1995.

COMPUTER CONNECTIONS

Library of Michigan's website http://www.libofmich.lib.mi.us

Secretary of State's office online http://www.sos.state.mi.us/

Detroit News Online http://detnews.com/politics/

Michigan Historical Museum and nine other museums that are part of the Michigan Historical Center http://www.sos.state.mi.us/history/history.html

VIDEOTAPES

The Islander. Beverly Hills, CA: New Star Video, 1988. 99 minutes. Story of young Inga, who grows up in the man's world of commercial fishing in the freezing waters of Lake Michigan.

Michigan. Produced by Milwaukee, WI: Raintree Publishers. Distributed by New York: Ambrose Video, 1987. 49 minutes.

AUDIOTAPES/COMPACT DISCS

Hitsville U.S.A.: The Motown Singles Collection, 1959–1971. Los Angeles: Motown Record Corporation, 1992.

The Most-Played Oldies on America's Jukeboxes, by Motown's Greatest Artists. Hollywood, CA: Motown Record Corporation, 1987.

INDEX

Page numbers for illustrations, charts, and graphs, are in boldface.